RULE 1

Taking charge of the dominion mandate that God has given us

Published and Printed by:
Print on Demand, Parow, South Africa

ISBN: 978-0-620-84978-4 (Print)
ISBN: 978-0-620-84979-1 (e-book)

Acknowledgements

First of all we acknowledge our Great God who inspired us to do this work for the benefit of His Church.

Then our gratitude to the Haridien and Maritz families who prayed and supported us in seeing this work through. Your labours are not in vain in the Lord!

I would like to thank my brother in faith and friend, Richard Haridien, for his encouraging words and support in writing this book and for making this journey together. I am humbled to have been invited and be a part of this project. My wish and desire is that love dictates this endeavour. That is love from God and to God and our contemporaries. I sincerely hope that this book turns out to be the blessing to all that it is intended to be. From Andrew Maritz.

I thank Andrew Maritz for the special journey that God allowed us to make together by writing this book. Our minds and hearts just merged together by inspiration of the Holy Spirit. This book will be a blessing and inspiration to all that will read it. From Richard Haridien

Also special thanks to Diane Thompson who assisted us with the editing. Only with a keen, neutral and specialist eye could one acknowledge that there is always a better way to express oneself.

Lastly, a word of thanks to the Print on Demand Printing and Publishing team for your professional assistance.

Dedication

We dedicate this book to all the overcomers and rulers in the Church of Jesus Christ. May your rule be just, fair and powerful now and in eternity.

Further dedication to the Unborn who were not allowed to see the light of day for whatever reason.

Lastly, we dedicate this book to those who were afflicted and ravished by severe depression that ultimately led to suicide. May you receive special grace and mercy from our loving God.

About the Authors

Richard Haridien is an Evangelist, Author, Poet, Songwriter, Life Coach, Church Unifier, Inventor and Entrepreneur who lives in Cape Town, South Africa.

He is recently widowed when God called Lorraine, his late wife home after she suffered a severe stroke. She stepped into heaven on 14 April 2019. They are blessed with two adult sons who are both married and who, with God's grace, have provided four lovely grandchildren to the extended family.

Andrew Maritz is a priest as well as a qualified IT Technician. He has served in the ministry for 22 years and resides in Cape Town, South Africa where he is still actively serving in the Priestly ministry. Andrew also lived and worked in Scotland and England for 15 years in various industries and sectors.

He is married to Martha, his wife of 14 years, and has been blessed with two daughters - Elektra and Emily as well as son Alexander.

Andrew enjoys sport, music, the outdoors and anything that can pleasantly surprise. His passion is the workings of Jesus Christ.

List of Contents:

Prologue

Parts:

1. Self (control over own thoughts, emotions and speech/conduct);

2. Family (marital and familial relationships);

3. Environment/Community/Mission – dominion over/responsibility for;

4. Work/Business/Investments (reigning/ruling over);

5. Ultimately in New Jerusalem/Kingdom of God.

Epilogue

Notes:

Biblical and other references.

Prologue

"To him who overcomes I will grant to sit
with Me on My throne, as I also
overcame and sat down with My Father
on His throne"[1]

The above-mentioned Bible word is very powerful indeed! It is a reference to sitting on a throne. And not just *any* throne. It is the authority and privilege that Jesus will confer upon the overcomers. This authority and privilege will come at the end after they overcame everything that was placed in their path of faith and life. They became overcomers by faith in Jesus Christ, as well as through their unwavering trust in Him and His grace.

To be able to sit with Jesus on His throne means that they will also rule with Him in a delegated fashion as He pleases. Just to clarify – they will not sit with Jesus on His own and self-same throne. But they will be given similar types of thrones – albeit of lesser significance and import – like the one He is sitting on. The image of thrones in this instance refers to *why* they will be sitting on His throne(s) and *what* they would be doing whilst sitting on those thrones.

It is expected that those overcomers will rule the new earth as delegates in the name and power of Jesus, as He has found them worthy to do that.

By delegated rule, it is automatically assumed that the authority will have its limits as prescribed by Jesus Himself. What that delegated rule will involve no one knows yet, and will not know until it has been awarded to the overcomers. Jesus has ALL authority in heaven and on earth. The overcomers will enjoy limited rule and authority assigned to them.

One can see it when one looks at the justice system of a country. You have a judge that rules in a lower court (like a magistrate's court). That judge has authority to exercise judgement and has limited sentencing authority (for instance: the maximum sentence he can ascribe to a person convicted of a crime is 10 years). If the crime is of such a nature that the sentence would likely be more than the maximum he could give, the matter is escalated to a higher court. Thus, in certain countries, that higher court would be a regional court. An even higher court can be a high or supreme court. But even beyond that, a higher court could be an appeals court or the constitutional court.

The Apostle James says:

> "Blessed is the man who endures temptation; for when he has been approved, he will receive the crown of life which the Lord has promised to those who love Him."[2]

The 'crown of life' also has reference to the ultimate reign of God's people in the eternal heavens. The crown also alludes to an image of what could be described as 'the best' or 'the highest' that one can find. In this instance, the 'crown of life' could also refer to the best or highest life that one can find. That life is eternal life in glory with God.

This will be the ultimate privilege and authority given to man. These human beings will be much more than normal men (or women). They will be perfected and godly heavenly beings enabled by God to perform the work that He assigns to them. That assignment will entail the eternal ruling and reigning over territories (or cities) that will form part of the new earth (heaven) that will never come to an end. The concept of ruling over cities could likewise also be the authority over all sorts of territories (geographical or otherwise). Look what Jesus said in the parable of the minas:

> "And he said to him, 'Well done, good servant; because you were faithful in a very little, have authority over ten cities".[3]

All the above relates to what will happen at the end when the new earth and heavens are established together with the New Jerusalem. That is good to know and worthwhile to strive towards.

But in the meantime, there is much work that needs to be done. In the meantime, we must fulfil God's mandate to have dominion over the earth in what He said to man:

> "Be fruitful and multiply; fill the earth *and subdue it; have dominion (rule) over* the fish of the sea, over the birds of the air, and over every living thing that moves on the earth"[4] [Emphasis added].

This godly mandate for man over the natural creation also extends to dominion over the spiritual things. Remember what God told Cain *before* he murdered his brother:

"If you do well, will you not be accepted? And if you do not do well, sin lies at your door. And its desire is for you, but you should *rule over it*"[5] [Emphasis added].

It is thus clear that God wants us as His children to rule as His ambassadors in the natural, as well as the spiritual realms. The ruling should also extend to all spheres of life, even *having control over* our thoughts, emotions, speech and conduct. He further expects us to exercise control and to rule firmly, yet fairly, within our own families, the communities and environments, our finances and investments as well as within the Church of Jesus Christ. It is good to have control over certain things in our lives – and we should do that to order our lives better. But it is also wise to realize that there are certain things that we will never have any control over – things that are simply 'beyond our control'. In those instances, we draw on the help and support of our Lord and Saviour, Jesus Christ. But the things that we must do, we must do!

Within the Church of Jesus Christ, we must be careful not to lord over the believers. On the contrary, we should rather be servant leaders as Jesus gave us His example. We all remember how Jesus washed the feet of His disciples.

God, the King, rules supreme. This sounds like an understatement. Let me put it in another way. God, the Almighty is the King. And not just *any* king, but the King of kings! God rules from eternity to eternity in full authority. He is unrivalled, omnipotent, all-knowing, all-powerful, fully just and righteous, fully holy and complete. The Psalmist said this of God's kingdom:

"Your kingdom is an everlasting kingdom. And your dominion (rule) endures throughout all generations."[6]

God's rule is also supreme and sovereign. What does this mean? It means whatever God thinks, wills, and purposes, so it WILL be done. God does not have to consult anyone before He does anything. He does whatever pleases Him in whatever way He wishes and when He wishes. God has also already chosen His people whom He will save from eternal damnation and give them entry into His eternal kingdom.

However, after the victory through the cross over death and sin, Jesus received ALL authority due to this supreme sacrifice. He is allowed to sit at the right hand of God and is in charge of ruling the universe and ALL worlds. He is the One who wants to confer reign, rule and authority to His people – the overcomers and righteous ones. His conferring of reign and rulership to His own is simply a godly privilege – something we do not deserve and are not entitled to.

Although we are expected to rule and reign already here on earth, we should do it with the utmost humbleness and in full knowledge of this huge responsibility.

Jesus is the true example and epitome of humility and meekness. How we go about doing that is very important. Ultimately it will be our faith in God and partaking in the redeeming grace that Jesus offers, as well as being sanctified by God's Spirit, that will first allow us to be saved. This will be followed by a period of rule where those who have experienced salvation in Christ will reign as kings and priests with and through the life and power of the Redeemer and God. The thought of it is frightening to the human mind but deeply humbling when viewed from a godly perspective.

There is another angle to the topic of this book. *Rule 1* also alludes to a set of rules. People do not necessarily like the idea of rules. However, to respect rules is the duty and prerogative of human beings. Rules (or laws, regulations, obligations) assist us greatly in ordering our human existence. It helps us to make sense of our environment and respect our fellow human beings in how we conduct ourselves vis-à-vis the rules and safety of our neighbours. To follow rules brings about a measure of security and safety within society. It tells drivers to stop at an intersection where there is a red traffic light, indicating that we should do it. It enforces laws aligned to the ten commandments instituted by God long ago, which are respected by many cultures and societies. The main godly rule (law) that Jesus introduced and highlighted is almost a summary of the ten commandments. He said the following when questioned by the Pharisees:

> "You shall love the Lord your God with all your soul, and with all your heart, and with all your mind. This is the first and great commandment. And the second is like it: You shall love your neighbour as yourself. On these two commandments hang all the Law and the Prophets."[7]

This book will help us recognise the weight of the mandate of reigning and ruling as God's representatives already now in the places and spaces wherein God has placed us and we find ourselves.

He wants us to practise doing it now. See this as a practice run for our eternal reign and rule.

Enter our domain.

Part One
Ruling Self

Chapter 1
Individual ruler through thoughts

Man is the crown of God's creation. That is how He intended it right from the beginning. We know that God declared His work as 'good' after it was brought into existence. This good creation was also very beautiful and diverse in the sense that many creatures were from different groups and categories (i.e. plants, trees, grass, mountains, valleys, rivers, fountains, oceans, fish, birds, animals, etc.). Amazingly, the earth was built from the outside in. God started with the firmament – or the heavens as we know it – perfectly contradicting the way humans build, from the ground upwards. This diversity amongst groups of living things was also further divided into individual entities and creatures which were distinct on their own within their allotted groupings.

The human being, Adam, was the crown creation over every created thing. He was indeed excellent and, in status, just a little lower than angels.

The characteristics of this crowning and excellence included abilities and capabilities which were designed to be evident in the makeup and DNA of the human being.

Thus, the dominion that God has mandated Adam to have over all creation will be dealt with in later chapters of this book. However, this first chapter will focus on dominion and control of the human being over himself – i.e. his thoughts, intelligence, emotions, speech and behaviour as an internal mechanism of control. This touches on the inner man and experiences of self.

These abilities and capabilities of thoughts, intelligence and speech are innate and peculiar to the human race. These are some of the things that separate humans from other living creatures. These abilities allow humans to rule over other living creatures, as they can interact, plan, design and implement various schemes and projects. Humans can utilise materials and produce tools and implements to create further innovations and products that would otherwise not be brought into existence if left solely to animals. Animals are not in a position to do this and to step into a higher level of functioning. They are meant to just live to survive and to maintain themselves by partaking of food and drink from their environment.

Thus, humans are also creative but their creativity is subject to the use of materials and substances that were already created by God from nothing.

The creativity of human beings is one element of the 'image of God' into which humans were created that set them apart from all other living things.

Thoughts are powerful impulses and energies that allow human beings to evaluate facts, materials, tests of durability and strength, statistics, past successes and failures and to analyse and compare it with the vision of improvements and innovations. This flows into an abstract domain to visualise concrete structures and designs on the one hand as well as figurative reasonings on the other hand. Carefully considered thoughts can also provide human beings with the abilities to plan and execute strategies to conquer and overcome animals or other human beings in an attempt to capture or kill them.

Human beings can think creatively, thus using their thoughts for enjoyment and the common good. Here a person thinks of the fine arts, refined music, poetry and classical writings and documents, architecture, the building of towns and cities, transport systems, etc. for the records and perpetuation of culture. However, creative thinking could also be used for destructive purposes. In this regard, the fall of man into sin gave rise to those thoughts. Thus, what God has created and built up (also with the intervention of human beings) could be destroyed by wrongful thinking and sentiments.

Thought also touches onto the spiritual side. Faith is the way for human beings to come to God. However, it is also expected that they think and make decisions to obey and serve God.

The Apostle Paul mentions a range of spiritual fruit that a child of God should aspire to inculcate into their souls and spiritual makeup. He says in Galatians:

> "But the fruit of the Spirit is love, joy, peace, longsuffering, gentleness, goodness, faith, meekness, *temperance*: against such there is no law"[8] [Emphasis added].

The ninth fruit of the Spirit is temperance or 'self-control'. In the New International Version (NIV) of the Bible, the word 'temperance' is changed to 'self-control'. This entire chapter of the book will focus on the concept of self-control. Self-control is not a bad thing. Indeed, it is very good as it forms part of the nine noted fruit of the Spirit. In modern literature and thinking, the word 'control' is viewed in a negative connotation. It is not meant to be that way.

During colonialism and other periods of conquests, the military superior forces conquered and dominated weaker nations or peoples with limited military prowess. This domination and control were viewed in a negative light, as the dominated nations had limited rights and privileges.

However, the word 'control' can also have more positive connotations. This is where control over situations or circumstances could lead to improvements in living conditions through appropriate legislation and rules. It could furthermore lead to a fairer distribution and maintenance of resources and assets that ensure such resources to be utilised for many years into the future. Thus, conversely, a lack of proper control could bring about depletion of resources and assets in a relatively short period of time.

This spiritual fruit of self-control is meant to help the individual exercise restraint and discretion in how he/she conducts him-/herself in everyday life.

Everything for the human being starts with his/her thoughts. From there it finds expression either through speech or actions or a combination thereof.

We can have good or bad thoughts.

Good thoughts can centre on creativity, positivity, increase, improvements, building up, support, encouragement, implementation, inclusion, victory and celebration.

Bad thoughts can focus on destruction, negativity, decrease, breaking down, discouragement, failure, exclusion, envy, jealousy and hatred.

As Christians, we are called to self-control in order to conduct ourselves in a worthy and Christlike manner. Good thoughts should emanate from us that would be constructive and pleasing for ourselves, our neighbour and our God.

Good thoughts can lead to the support and building of the Church of Jesus Christ. Good thoughts also colour and direct our prayer-life and speech.

King Solomon says in one of his proverbs:

> "For as a man thinks in his heart, so is he."[9]

A wise man once said: "You cannot keep birds from flying over your head but you can keep them from building a nest in your hair".

The words of this wise man centre around the thoughts that are comparable with a bird in this instance. Human beings have thousands of thoughts each day. However, only some thoughts stick if you entertain them and give them space in your head.

Thoughts are also comparable with a busy highway in the head. Traffic of all sorts is moving in both directions all the time. You have large and massive vehicles, such as trucks, buses, those that carry abnormal loads and also cars of every shape and colour, even motorbikes. Many thoughts come to us each day of our lives. It takes dedication and focus to concentrate on a few good thoughts. However, we are exhorted by the Apostle Paul to do this in the following way:

> "Finally, brethren, whatever things are true, whatever things are noble, whatever things are just, whatever things are lovely, whatever things are of good report, if there is any virtue and if there is anything praiseworthy – meditate on these things."[10]

This is the secret: meditate on these things. Think about it; focus on it. Let such thoughts and matters occupy our thought lives.

Special thoughts and wishes from a dear friend:

Allow me to dedicate this section as a tribute to my long-time friend, Gustav Cookson.

I was born and bred in Kensington, Cape Town, South Africa during the 'Apartheid' government regime of the white majority National Party. The apartheid laws regulated separate development of the different racial and cultural groups and communities in the country. Those years were not easy if you did not belong to the white population group. It indicated where you must live, work, worship in church, who to have intimate relationships with, get married to, where you must sit in public transportation vehicles, which public ablution facilities you could use, which beaches you could swim at, etc. I also hated those evil laws and participated as a high school student in public demonstrations. Fortunately, with the public resistance and struggle against those laws, eventually, a new black multiparty government was inaugurated on 27 April 1994, and its first democratically elected black president was Nelson Mandela.

I met Gustav Cookson and his family in 1975, as I was called to attend a new local church congregation. The Cookson family also lived a few streets away from where we used to live. Both Gustav and I were still teenagers, but we formed a close friendship that lasted many years.

Even though my family that reared me, my uncle and aunt Freddy and Susan Jacobs, bought another house and we moved to a distant suburb, my friendship with Gustav continued. Our friendship even extended beyond both our separate marriages. Gustav, unfortunately, experienced difficulties in his first marriage which later ended. The same happened to his second marriage. He was again married for the third time! But, throughout his different marriages, the two of us maintained our friendship that also involved his other blended families.

However, something happened during his third marriage relating to our friendship that I do not understand. An unfortunate misunderstanding resulted in our friendship suffering. We started to drift apart.

Thereafter, I accepted a job offer in the United Kingdom and we emigrated to England as a family. All contact between Gustav and myself was completely broken. We lived in England for about seven years after which we decided to move back to South Africa during 2008.

However, even though we were back in the country, there was still no contact between Gustav and me.

Things started to change since early 2015.

I decided to attend a divine service with my wife, Lorraine, in a congregation in Rocklands, Mitchells Plain, Cape Town to see another friend of ours who was ordained into the priestly ministry.

During the divine service, I noticed that a younger brother of Gustav, Clarence Cookson, was also active in the ministry in that congregation.

After the service, I spoke with Clarence and asked how his brother was doing. He gave me Gustav's telephone number and asked if I would contact him. Apparently, Gustav had tried by all means to get back in contact with me without success.

When I phoned Gustav later in the day, he was overjoyed. I shared in the joyful reunion. We made arrangements to meet the following Saturday at a coffee shop in Mitchells Plain. The meeting was surreal and great.

Since that time, we met on a regular basis.

He told me he had contracted cancer a few years earlier that almost cost him his life. But, during that time of his struggle with cancer, he asked God to spare him to be able to see me again. He later learned that I had emigrated to England but kept asking and praying for a reunion. God healed him from cancer which went into remission. But still, there was no sign of me.

God moved my circumstances in such a way that my wife and I decided to move back to South Africa. But it still took a few years before God inspired me to attend the divine service in Rocklands. This led to my meeting with Gustav.

Unfortunately, only a week or two after our meeting, Gustav had a relapse and cancer returned with a vengeance. He became very sick and frail in a short time.

During one of my visits to his house, he told me that he loved church music. I also know that he was an avid tenor as well as a dedicated choir conductor in bygone years. He said he had loaded a large collection of church hymns on his phone to which he listened from time to time. On one occasion, while he was wringing in pain, he talked with God to help him. His phone tablet that was completely switched off at that point suddenly went on and started to play the second verse of a hymn that had three verses. The words of that second verse talked directly to his frame of mind and was an encouragement to him then. This kind of miraculous church music phenomenon occurred a number of times. When he told me, I believed him. After all, there is nothing that our God cannot do. Gustav had a very close and intimate relationship with God.

One day, God told me to give Gustav a money gift of cash that I placed in an envelope. When I gave it to him, he was very moved and said they needed the funds and prayed that God open a way for them. Both Gustav and his wife were unemployed and he was in receipt of a government disability grant. They also struggled financially. I asked him to offer a tenth (tithe) of that money gift the next day in church. He was so thankful for the suggestion and said he could not offer much during the recent past. The next day was also a special divine service of intercession for 'the departed souls'. The church celebrated three Sundays per year set aside for such special divine services.

Gustav's illness gripped him completely and thereafter he became bedridden.

The last time my wife and I visited him at his house was on a Sunday after we had attended a divine service in our own congregation that was conducted by Apostle Mark Diedericks. We were filled with great power and joy that we went to share with Gustav. I also read to him a special hymn that had impacted me during that service. It goes as follows:

"Why should we tarry when Jesus is pleading, pleading for you and for me? Why should we linger and heed not His mercies, mercies for you and for me? Come home, come home. Ye who are weary, come home. Earnestly, tenderly, Jesus is calling, calling 'O sinner, come home'".[11]

When I read that verse, Gustav was inwardly moved and shaken. He looked deeply into my eyes and just nodded. I could feel that he was ready to go home to Jesus and to heed His call.

Not long after this encounter, Gustav was graciously called home during August 2015 to take up his place in heaven.

I cannot say why God decided to call Gustav home to heaven at the time that He did. But I am convinced that it was a far better option than for him to remain in this earthly life. Even Apostle Paul was torn between the two options: "I am pulled in two directions. I want very much to leave this life and be with Christ, which is a far better thing" Philippians 1:23 (Good News Translation).

Now I have another close friend in heaven. It's now quite a large cloud of witnesses that I have there, I must say. I am glad that God heeded Gustav's prayer to extend his life after the first time he had contracted cancer because he wanted to see me again and reconcile. God has granted his wish and crowned those thoughts with goodness and blessing.

Chapter 2
Individual ruler through emotions

"An emotion is a feeling such as happiness, love, fear, anger or hatred, which can be caused by the situation that you are in or the people you are with."[12]

In the 20th century, Paul Ekman identified six basic emotions (anger, disgust, fear, happiness, sadness, and surprise). Robert Plutchik identified eight which he grouped into four pairs of polar opposites (joy-sadness, anger-fear, trust-distrust, surprise-anticipation).

When looking at the complex nature of human beings, one is amazed at how much we are endowed with. Besides the obvious physical part, there is also the abstract or invisible part touching on our thoughts, emotions, values, beliefs, drives, passions and desires which could overlap, but also stand on their own. All this is also influenced by our life experiences, conditions and situations of our background and upbringing. Let's also add to the equation the impact of teaching and socialization from our parents and other individuals and mentors who have directly or inadvertently touched our lives.

Emotions are one of those areas of our lives that distinguish us from animals and other life forms. Yes, we do have feelings.

Feelings are not bad in themselves. However, it is how we manage the many feelings or emotions that we encounter from time to time that determine our lives and the quality of our lives.

We should also rule over our emotions. How do we do that? Emotions or feelings can be very powerful when they flood through us.

Scripture tells us that even Jesus Christ experienced a range of human emotions from time to time that was appropriate during certain situations. Just think of some of the following situations just to mention a few:

> **Anger:** "When He had made a whip of cords, He drove them all out of the temple, with the sheep and the oxen, and poured out the changers' money and overturned the tables."[13]

> **Compassion:** "But when He saw the multitudes, He was moved with compassion for them, because they were weary and scattered, and like sheep having no shepherd."[14]

The above are just two examples of how Jesus went about also experiencing the gamut of human emotions. At other times *He simply wept!*

He *also rejoiced* (was glad) in many things and people if it flowed in union with His Father's will. Jesus was fully God and fully human. He did not stand aloof looking in and talking down to the ordinary man. However, He did not allow negative emotions to control Him or to move Him to do that which was against the will of God.

In the garden of Gethsemane, knowing full well what supreme sacrifice He had to make, He was *extremely sad*:

> "He began to be sorrowful and deeply distressed. Then He said to them, 'My soul is exceedingly sorrowful, even to death.'"[15]

In certain quarters (clinical psychology and psychiatry) this might be described as a bout of severe depression. Our hearts go out to our fellow human beings who experience incidents and moments (even days and weeks) of severe depression due to illness. Some of them respond well to chemotherapy and/or psychotherapy while others do not. Some never get out of such a dark place and commit suicide as the perceived 'only way out'. We pray that God covers them with His mercy and grace in eternity – that will remain His sovereign rule and no man or spirit can say anything against it.

However, Jesus was confronted with this severe calamity. A calamity that not only involved Himself, but also ALL mankind. The entire weight of SIN committed by all humanity, past, present and future, bore down on Him. He buckled under this pressure and weight in prayer and communication with His Father. What makes this moment in time so spectacular was the fact that Jesus foreknew what would happen. He knew that He had to go through it, even before He was born into this world. There is a heavy burden of foreknowledge. However, he decided to obey His Father's will in this regard and to drink this extremely bitter cup for the benefit of sinful man. Through His supreme sacrifice that will remain valid and effective for ALL time, sinful man was redeemed from sin because He took our transgressions upon Himself. He is the substitute that took the wrath of God and made us righteous and just before God. This is wonderful, good news indeed!

When it comes to us as human beings, it is expected that we experience a range of emotions from time to time that also moves us. It can lift us up or press us down.

In another Biblical sense, our emotions are referred to as our 'heart'. This is the innermost part of us that has all sorts of feelings, both good and bad. With reference to what is going on in our hearts, consider the following biblical texts:

> "*The heart is deceitful* above all things. And desperately wicked; who can know it? I, the Lord, search the heart, I test the mind, even to give every man according to his ways. According to the fruit of his doings."[16]

> "For *out of the heart proceed evil thoughts*, murders, adulteries, fornications, thefts, false witness, blasphemies. These are the things which defile a man..."[17]

Thus, what we can deduce from the above is the fact that although our hearts contain our emotions and feelings, it is very deceitful and unstable. If we are totally driven by our emotions alone, we will be on a crazy rollercoaster ride on a daily basis. Although it is fine that we do have emotions, it is also better that we try to control even some of the very destructive ones that come and go from time to time.

One sure way to attempt to do that is by allowing the peace of God to guard and rule our emotions. This can come about by seeking a very close relationship with God on a continuous basis.

Sure, we are allowed to experience anger as Jesus did. But we should not allow the anger to get the better of us. Anger should not stay or linger long as it could fester and lead to bitterness. The apostle Paul told the Ephesians:

> "Be angry, and do not sin: *do not let the sun go down on your wrath*, nor give place to the devil"[18] [Emphasis added].

Thus, we can and should experience all sorts of feelings as human beings but, as children of God, we have what our fellow human beings don't have: God's grace and help in need.

In the book of Proverbs, it says:

> "Keep (guard) your heart with all diligence, for out of it spring the issues of life."[19]

Even in the negative emotions such as fear, anxiety and worry, we do have an outcome that we can count on. Look at what Apostle Paul told the congregation at Philippi:

> "Be anxious for nothing, but in everything by prayer and supplication, with thanksgiving, let your requests be made known to God; and the peace of God, which surpasses all understanding, will *guard your hearts and minds* through Christ Jesus"[20] [Emphasis added].

God is so much greater than our hearts! He is also far greater than our emotions and will even help us in our striving to control our emotions and heart. We can trust God more than we can trust our hearts. "For if our hearts condemn us, God is greater than our heart, and knows all things" (1 John 3:20). And this trust goes for all kinds of emotions, the positive and good ones as well as the negative and not so good ones. It stabilizes the pendulum in our favour.

Do you know that God is even interested in our feelings? He, the Almighty God, cares how we feel. When Cain was focused on himself and contemplating to take a certain kind of action, God approached him by saying:

> "Why are you angry? And why is your countenance fallen?"[21]

The great God saw the face and heart of Cain, that it was angry as well as 'fallen', meaning that he was sad and depressed. And God stepped in after He saw Cain's disposition and gave him some sound advice – which Cain obviously ignored.

It also helps us to rule with wisdom and kindness what goes on in our hearts and emotions. Remember, although our thoughts can inspire and motivate us, it's our emotions that are powerful and an energised driver into sure action that finds expression in our conduct and behaviour. Apostle Paul also advises the Colossians:

> "And let the peace of God *rule in your hearts*, to which also you were called in one body; and be thankful"[22] [Emphasis added].

Chapter 3
Individual ruler through speech and conduct

What is normally born as a thought develops sometimes into a powerful emotion (positive or negative). It ultimately develops further into speech and how we conduct ourselves.

Our thoughts and feelings are mainly private matters that happen within us. However, if we pay close attention, our feelings can sometimes be 'read' by others through our body language and actions. If we feel sad or depressed, our facial expressions, as well as our bending body structure, would tell a powerful story of what might be going on inside us. The same could be said of disappointments, joy, excitement, happiness and other emotions.

However, our speech is also a powerful tool, given to us by God, which can be used to express ourselves and make our thoughts known to others.

With verbal speech, we can also nowadays add written speech through letters (whether handwritten or typed), emails, WhatsApp or other messages via social media. Very few people take the trouble to write letters by hand anymore or even post them via the slow mail system.

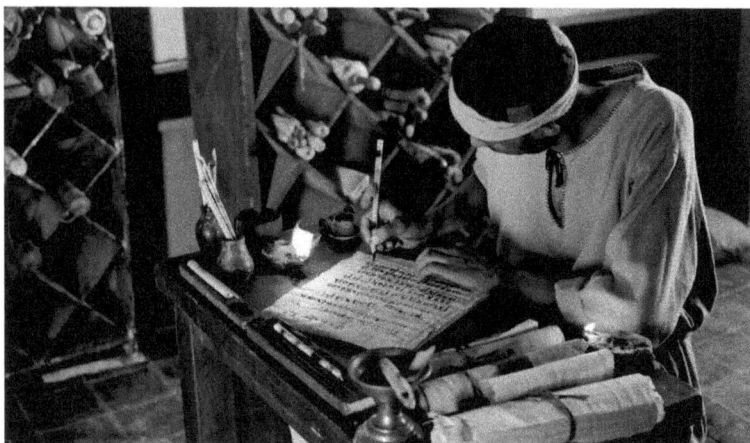

As much as we should be careful of what we think and feel, we must be even more careful about our choice of words – verbally or otherwise.

A wise man once said: "Thoughts are like threads, speech like ropes, and deeds like chains."

As we can see, the progression from thoughts to speech, and later through deeds, just becomes stronger and more binding.

The Bible teaches us:

> "Let your speech always be with grace, seasoned with salt, that you may know how you ought to answer each one."[23]

Yes, indeed, we should talk with much grace and seasoning! How we communicate to our family, colleagues, neighbours or anyone else, is important. Our words are very powerful. They can build up or destroy. Our responsibility is to talk life into our fellow man, especially our own family.

Remember that, through God's Word, the entire creation and universe came into being. We should also rule over our speech.

Apostle James put it so nicely:

> "Indeed, we put bits in horses' mouths that they may obey us, and we turn their whole body. Look also at ships: although they are so large and are driven by fierce winds, they are turned by a small rudder wherever the pilot desires. Even so, the tongue is a little member and boasts great things."[24]

God's children are to use their mouths to praise Him. They also use their mouths to testify about the gospel of Christ and bring the testimony of His grace and salvation to many lost ones. We should not use the same mouths to create havoc and be destructive. We should rule wisely over our speech and utterances.

Let us speak truth.
Let us speak life.
Let us speak healing.
Let us speak wonders.
Let us speak abundance.
Let us speak deliverance.
Let us speak miracles.
Let us speak holiness.
Let us speak godliness.

Let us speak such things to edify and build one another up.

Speak upliftment and positivity into our families and the Church!

Apostle Paul admonishes the Ephesians concerning their speech and to not grieve the Holy Spirit as follows:

"Let no *corrupt word proceed out of your mouth*, but what is good for necessary edification, that it may impart grace to the hearers. And do not grieve the Holy Spirit of God, by whom you were sealed for the day of redemption. Let all bitterness, wrath, anger, clamour, *and evil speaking be put away from you*, with all malice. And be kind to one another, tender-hearted, forgiving one another, even as God in Christ forgave you"[25] [Emphasis added].

The ultimate progression from thoughts, emotions and speech leads one into action. It culminates in our conduct and behaviour.

We ought to conduct ourselves in a worthy manner as children of the Highest God. The way we carry ourselves should speak volumes of who we are as the royal priesthood and future kings and rulers. God equips and empowers His own through His Spirit. God gives us the necessary authority, power, gifts and abilities to have control over ourselves and our environment.

Look how Apostle Paul admonished his protégé, Timothy:

"A bishop then must be blameless, the husband of one wife, temperate, sober-minded, *of good behaviour*, hospitable, able to teach, not given to wine, not violent, not greedy for money, but gentle, not quarrelsome, not covetous; one who rules his house well, having his children in submission with all reverence (for if a man does not know how to rule his house, how will he take care of the church of God?); not a novice, lest being puffed up with pride he fall into the same condemnation as the devil. Moreover, he must have a good testimony among those who are outside, lest he fall into reproach and the snare of the devil"[26] [Emphasis added].

What a resume for a bishop! Sure, we cannot all be bishops, but we will do well if we take notice of this admonition as it equally applies to the behaviour and standard of all God's children.

Our conduct must be our real testimony of the gospel of Christ. Thus, without words, we can show the way for lost souls to the gate of heaven. Apostle Paul also advises the Romans to present their bodies as living sacrifices to God:

"I beseech you therefore, brethren, by the mercies of God, that you *present your bodies a living sacrifice, holy, acceptable to God*, which is your reasonable service. And do not be conformed to this world, but be transformed by the renewing of your mind, that you may prove what is that good and acceptable and perfect will of God"[27] [Emphasis added].

Lastly, concerning our conduct and way of living, Apostle Paul tells the congregation of the Corinthians:

"Therefore, having these promises beloved, let us cleanse ourselves from all filthiness of the flesh and spirit, perfecting holiness in the fear of God."[28]

Heavenly speech through prayer (by Andrew Maritz)

Prayer is a powerful gift that we all possess. Its weight is not carried in how eloquently we speak but in how sincere we are when praying. The sincere prayer of an innocent child can do more wonders than the well-worded prayer of a church minister.

It is not the mind but the heart that matters. After all, we are having a heart to heart with our heavenly Father.

I was blessed to be taught at an early age to pray by my Dad and Sunday school teachers. At first, I had the same nervousness and anxiety, as do many, to pray in front of others. I sometimes was laughed at for saying something out of context. I was once asked by my Dad to pray before he went out to do his ministerial work. I was 12 years old and asked the Lord to bless the brothers who go to do His missionary work instead of asking God to bless my Dad. After I was done praying and opened my eyes, everyone was laughing. It got better over time.

As a child, my prayers were simple and to the point. It was to help in my school exams and for God's protection over my family and for His blessing. At church, I would listen to how the preachers prayed and copied them. We pray for our meals and before we head off to church. It is also good to pray first thing in the morning and at night before bedtime.

Why is prayer so important and why do we pray?

Let's look at the best example: Jesus Christ. Prayer was an integral part of His life here on earth. He often prayed before big events occurred. Remember the raising of Lazarus from the dead and before His own crucifixion. It was in prayer that He connected with God the Father. His prayers were heartfelt and in reverence to the Father. He spoke to God as if His essence was the life that everything hinges on. We do the very same thing. We connect with the Almighty and with an open heart. There is nothing we can hide from Him anyway. Thus, we always approach the Father with reverence and humbleness. We always bring our thankfulness and gratitude to God first. Then we pray for others. Lastly, we pray for ourselves.

Prayer is to the soul what breathing is to the body. It connects the soul with the Divine life of its Creator. When we pray and ask for God's help, we cannot doubt that He can or will help. Prayer needs to be filled with conviction and faith. This conviction is embodied in the 'amen' we say at the end of it. 'Amen' means 'yes, so shall it be'. We cannot ask for God's help and then not have faith. Without faith, it is impossible to please God.

As much as God answers prayers – in His will and time – He may also not answer our prayers. This does not mean we should give up praying when they are not answered straight away. Jesus teaches that we must persist in our prayers even if they are not answered immediately. God can see the bigger picture in our lives that we cannot see. Time as we know it does not affect life as He made it. He lives the past, present and future all in one. Therefore, our prayers are filled with trust in His judgment. He will answer all prayers that are in line with His will and will always do what is right for our future fellowship with Him.

Jesus also taught not to pray as an outer show but to do it in private. He teaches us to go into our inner room, close the door behind us and then pray. We can do this wherever we are. We can shut ourselves off from our surroundings and quietly pray from our heart without uttering a word. Similarly, we can do this when doing confession and while celebrating Holy Communion. There is, however, nothing wrong with the tradition of going on our knees and praying. In fact, this is also a symbol of our humbleness and total dependence on God.

Scripture teaches that God will always grant the requests in prayer that are in line with His divine will – that He will not reject a thankful heart. Also, prayer made in Jesus' Name or for Jesus' sake will be acknowledged. However, Jesus taught us to be persistent in prayer. God already knows what is in our hearts and minds before we even ask anything. He advised us to keep knocking on God's door to the point where He answers just to stop the constant knocking. In so doing, this wonderful vehicle that connects us with the divine is highlighted. Prayer transcends space and time and thus the universe. By praying, we are already having intimate fellowship God.

What we pray about depends on how big our hearts are. We can speak to the Father about how our day is going. We can ask Him to help grow a little vegetable garden. We can ask Him to guide governments and give wisdom to our leaders. We can ask for help in making decisions. We can ask for direction in dealing with the difficult issues and problems that exist in countries across the globe. By praying, we unburden ourselves and place the things that we don't have control over into God's mighty Hand. "Lord, help!" – in these two words are already the makings of a short, yet significant, prayer.

Praise and thanksgiving should, however, be at the forefront of our minds when talking to our Father. In His sermon on the Mount (Matthew 5), Jesus taught His disciples and followers to first bring praise and worship to God when they prayed. Known today as *The Lord's Prayer*, this prayer includes everything we need for body, soul and spirit. We can thank God for just about everything – His love, grace, goodness, kindness, mercy, Jesus, His Holy Spirit, His angels' protection, family and loved ones, gifts, talents, strength, health, blessings, successes, food, the seasons and so forth.

The list is endless.

By praying we connect and engage the Divine. It strengthens our relationship with God. It brings comfort and peace to the soul. Give this gift to the children. Teach them to pray.

Part Two
Ruling the Family

Chapter 4
Marital Relationships

According to the UN in 2019, the country with the highest divorce rate in the world is the Maldives with 10.97 divorces per 1,000 inhabitants per year. This is followed by Belarus with 4.63 and the United States with 4.34.

Rank	Country	Divorces per 1,000 inhabitants per year
1	Maldives	10.97
2	Belarus	4.63
3	United States	4.34
4	Cuba	3.72
5	Estonia	3.65
6	Panama	3.61
7	Puerto Rico	3.61
8	Ukraine	3.56

| 9 | Russia | 3.42 |
| 10 | Antigua and Barbuda | 3.40^{29} |

This is a stark reality. About 1% of all marriages in a country with the Maldives ends in divorce. This figure is cascaded to all other countries. And this figure escalates even higher if one takes into account that not all broken marriages end up in an official divorce. Some marriages just cease to exist. The couple just drifts apart without even going to the divorce courts.

The recent royal wedding between Prince Harry and Meghan Markle casts the spotlight on fairy-tale weddings. Images of a young couple who are madly in love and vow to spend the rest of their lives together, filled with expectations of a perfect marriage, are what fairy-tale weddings are made of.

The truth is that not all marriages end up being the stereotypical fairy tale we know and love. In fact, 25 326 divorces were granted in South Africa in 2016. This is according to a recently released report by Statistics South Africa on marriages and divorces.

Unfortunately, a high proportion of couples will have a 'happily ever after' that lasts less than 10 years. Results showed that four in ten divorces (44,4%) of the 25 326 in 2016 were marriages that lasted for less than 10 years.[30]

This is worrisome! That means almost half of all marriages end up in divorce in South Africa. I'm sure that is also the case in many other countries.

Why do we want to talk about the matter of divorce in a chapter dealing with the marital relationship? Because the two matters are intertwined.

It is very important to work on the marital relationship. If we neglect to do that, it has a greater probability to fail than if we work hard to keep it going. It is like tending the proverbial garden. If you don't work diligently in the garden, it will deteriorate and shrivel in neglect.

We believe that the couple in the marital relationship are equal partners – not the same, but equal. They are supposed to augment each other. That is the way God has instituted marriage – for the union of one man and one woman. However, the scripture says that the man is the head and, as the head, he should take the lead. Because men and women are different physiologically, emotionally and how they view and approach things in life, they bring variety and colour to the relationship. They see things from a different perspective and communicate those differences to each other. The trick is for the couple to listen and to respect each other. This is how love should grow and prosper.

Apostle Paul says to the Ephesians:

> "For this reason, a man shall leave his father and mother and be joined to his wife, and the two shall become one flesh...let each one of you in particular so love his own wife as himself, and let the wife see that she respects her husband."[31]

It is further stated in Hebrews:

> "Marriage is honourable among all, and the bed undefiled"[32]

Thus, it is clear that God who instituted marriage right from the beginning of human existence, when he introduced Adam and Eve to each other, wants human beings to love and nurture each other in a unified bond of marriage. This is to be found on the basis of love and respect for each other and the different roles and responsibilities coming to bear of both. Every husband needs his wife and every wife needs her husband. They complement and augment each other. They fit snugly together just as God intended it to be within a marriage.

Yes, the challenges, conflicts, demands and complexities are far more difficult for us in these modern times than that of Adam and Eve, or even for many centuries past affecting our forebears. However, if we do what we are advised through scripture and build our marital relationship on a daily basis, God's grace will cover us and He will help us to sustain our marital relationships.

We are also bombarded with many other challenges presented to us in this modern-day and age through the so-called 'culture'. The notion that marriage could be changed to include people of the same sex or a range of other linkages should not deter us to hold fast to that which God has initially instituted and that which is right for the human race and God's people.

Let us take a look at a vision that Daniel received:

> "The fourth beast shall be a fourth kingdom on earth, which shall be different from all other kingdoms and shall devour the whole earth, trample it and break it in pieces…He shall speak pompous words against the Most High, shall persecute the saints of the Most High, and *shall intend to change times and law*. Then the saints shall be given into his hand for a time and times and half a time. But the court shall be seated, and they shall take away his dominion, to consume and destroy it forever. Then

the kingdom and dominion, and the greatness of the kingdoms under the whole heaven, shall be given to the people, the saints of the Most High. His kingdom is an everlasting kingdom, and all dominions shall serve and obey Him"[33] [Emphasis added].

The devil wants to break down what God builds up. The same can be said of marriages. The devil and his scoundrels will even try to change the times and law. Another meaning hereof is that they might (will) try to change the composition and definition of the marital godly institution by changing legislation and policy in favour of new and alternative ways of seeing marriage. The good news is that even though they might be successful here and there to achieve it, God will ultimately intervene to enforce the correct godly law!

Let us do our utmost to preserve the sanctity of the marital relationship. Let us work on our marriages. Let us infuse love and respect into the marital bonds. Let us care for each other. In this way, we rule well. This is the kind of ruling pertaining to our marriages that God has placed into our hands to take responsibility for.

Let us remain faithful in our marriages.

Jesus said that if we are faithful in a few things (as in our marriages), He will make us ruler over many things!

Personal, miraculous manifestations

Early in my marriage to Lorraine, God allowed me to experience a few very traumatic incidents, as follows:

God loves us and only has thoughts of peace for us, to give us a future and a hope.

On a personal level, I was fortunate to have experienced God's protection on many occasions. One such occasion took place in July 1984 in Johannesburg, South Africa.

I was on my way by bus that particular morning to a work meeting in an area named Alexandra. It was raining heavily. When I stepped off the bus at my stop, there were quite a few people waiting to board the bus. Since it was still raining hard, I thought to cross the road in front of the bus. It was still stationary and it seemed as though there was no traffic approaching from either side.

As I walked past the bus and reached the middle of the busy main street, I was struck by a powerful 1000cc motorbike in full speed and flipped into mid-air. When I landed back onto the tar road, the force and impact made me slide face down on the road. I momentarily lost consciousness when my body stopped sliding. However, that did not remain for long as the cold and fierce rainfall kept me awake. Unfortunately, I could not move any part of my body as it was temporarily paralyzed from the impact and shock.

Miraculously, no vehicular traffic travelled on that part of the road at that point in time from either side, although it was normally a busy main street. Some people who witnessed the accident used their initiative to stop the traffic that started to move again with gusto.

Not long afterwards, a traffic officer was also on the scene and called for an ambulance.

An unknown lady approached by bowing down to talk with me lying quite still in the road. She asked if she could contact anyone from my family to inform them of the accident. I gave her my wife's (Lorraine's) name and work telephone number. This was some time before cellular phones.

The ambulance arrived after what seemed to me like hours. I was in excruciating pain with one leg broken at the knee, face swollen to twice its size and a few bruised ribs. The ambulance took me to the nearest health facility, Coronation Hospital. Soon after I arrived there, they further transferred me to Hillbrow Medical Clinic. After I was settled in there, Lorraine received a telephone call from the unknown lady who assisted me at the accident scene. Lorraine was already five months pregnant at that stage.

Fortunately, Lorraine's manager arranged for a driver to bring her to visit me at the Coronation Hospital. When she inquired about my admission, they informed her that they had no record of my having been admitted there. As she persisted that they double-check their records, a nurse came by who overheard the conversation and said that she thought a patient, who was in a road accident near Alexandra, did come in earlier. She went to fetch a plastic bag with my clothes drenched in blood to give to Lorraine. My wife almost fainted with shock, thinking that her husband had died.

When the nurse realized the confusion she had created, she said that Lorraine did not have to be unduly concerned because I was still alive. They had immediately transferred me to the private Hillbrow Medical Clinic, owing to the fact that my medical aid scheme made adequate allowances for special medical treatment.

You can obviously imagine how relieved Lorraine was upon hearing the latest news, eliminating such confusion. When Lorraine eventually saw me at the Hillbrow Medical Clinic and shared what had happened at the Coronation Hospital, we both had a hearty laugh.

But we were thankful that God had protected me from a severe injury, disability and even death. For the sake of the readers, I just want to say that I fully recovered and recuperated in next to no time after the accident.

On another occasion in September 1984, while we were still living in Johannesburg, I was travelling on the Golden Highway towards the City of Johannesburg. I was driving a new Toyota Sedan that belonged to the company where I was employed at that time. I was driving quite fast and was pressing to get back to the office before the end of business as I was normally travelling in a lift club with the chief executive officer of the company.

There were four lanes going in the same direction. The heavy rain had just stopped and the sun was coming out sharply. However, the road surface was still wet and slippery. As I travelled in the fastest lane (the right lane) the sharp sunlight that just broke through the clouds shone mischievously into my eyes. The road took a steady incline as it crossed over another freeway, the Francois Oberholzer Freeway. As the car in which I was travelling moved up towards the top of the bridge and flyover, without any warning it became uncontrollable. It was as if everything went into slow motion.

I tried to keep the car in the lane even though it was skidding from side to side and moving as if it had its own mind and will. I became conscious of the fact that there were many fast-moving cars in the lane behind, as well as in the three lanes on my left. I did not dare crash my car into any of those, as it would have produced a big pileup. As my car was also reaching the crest of the bridge, I also became aware that, if the car went over the railing, it would fall onto the Francois Oberholzer Freeway beneath.

Suddenly, I just saw a white light in front of me. I do not know how it happened, but I managed to steer the car to stay in the same lane and, as it reached the crest, to crash full-on into a solid concrete pillar that was fixed on the little island of the fork in the road. With the impact, the car simply folded around the pillar. All the windows shattered and splintered. The roof and sides of the car folded in the same way as a person would press an empty coke can. The car was a total write-off.

Many drivers pulled over to the side of the road where it was safe to do so. Many people thought there was no way the driver of the car that just crashed into the concrete pillar could survive the accident, judging the speed on impact and how the car looked thereafter. I know, because some of them told me afterwards.

I had no injuries at all. My shoulder slammed into the steering wheel and the splinters of the shattered front screen window showered over my head. But, essentially, I was not injured at all. I just struggled to open the driver's door which was jammed.

Not far away from the island on the fork of the road stood a breakdown truck – as if they were expecting accidents to happen there. The truck driver came to assist me. He asked permission to attach my car wreck to take to the scrap yard and also offered me a lift into town to drop me near my office.

When I stepped into the office, most of the staff had already left as it was just outside office hours. I went to the chief executive officer as she was waiting for me. I travelled with her in a lift club from where I used to live. When I saw her, I told her that I had just had a road accident and written off one of her company's new Toyotas. It looked as if she did not believe me at first. Then, when she realized that I was indeed serious, she asked if I was okay. She was not too concerned about the car. The more I told her I was indeed fine, the less she seemed to believe me. Later, I let her take me to the nearest hospital to have me medically checked and cleared. Maybe it was because I came across as unhurt and downplaying the traumatic incident, I don't know. Maybe she thought there was something wrong with my mind – or maybe she just wanted to check that I had no internal injuries that I might not be fully aware of.

However, the medical tests at the hospital gave me a good and clear report.

Once again, I experienced the protective Hand of God that brought me out of the probability of severe injury or death.

The Psalmist spoke about the angel of the Lord setting up camp around those who fear God:

"The angel of the Lord encamps all around those who fear Him, and delivers them" (Psalm 34:7).

We cannot see the angels, but it is enough that they can see us. There is one great Angel of the Covenant whom, not having seen, we love, and His Eye is always upon us both day and night. He has a host of holy ones under Him, and He causes these to be watchers over His saints and to guard them against all ill.

Note that the LORD of angels does not come and go and pay us transient visits, but He and His armies encamp around us. The headquarters of the army of salvation is where those live whose trust is in the living God. This camp surrounds the faithful so that they cannot be attacked from any quarter unless the adversary can break through the entrenchments of the LORD of angels.

We have a fixed protection, a permanent watch. Sentineled by the messengers of God, we shall not be surprised by sudden assaults nor swallowed up by overwhelming forces. Deliverance is promised in this verse. Deliverance by the great Captain of our salvation, and that deliverance we shall obtain again and again until our warfare is accomplished and we exchange the field of conflict for the home of rest.'[34]

Chapter 5
Familial Relationships

The family unit is the building blocks of society. From these building blocks, communities, towns, cities, regions, countries and the world community are hewn together.

"Family structure has changed dramatically over the last 50 years. The 'Leave it to Beaver' family is no longer the standard and several variations on the family have been created. There are six specific types of family structures identified by society today. The nuclear family is the traditional type of family structure. This family type consists of two parents and children. The nuclear family was long held in esteem by society as being the ideal in which to raise children. Children in nuclear families receive strength and stability from the two-parent structure and generally have more opportunities due to the financial ease of two adults.

According to 2010 U.S. Census data, almost 70 percent of children live in a nuclear family unit."[35]

The family unit could be as small as just two individuals (husband and wife) within a marital relationship. In modern culture, this definition of marriage is being redefined and, may I say with humility and respect, away from the godly institution of how God intended it to be from the very start.

A lot of problems will still be encountered as this 'redefined' marital unit is allowed to proceed into the future. Sure, there were also many problems within the traditional marital units of husband and wife. But, with this new redefinition, added problems unforeseen hereto will rear their ugly heads. This matter, however, falls outside the scope of this book.

So, out of a normal marital relationship, offspring comes forth by God's blessing. It is true that some families continue to function without children being born from their union – either by choice or biology. This situation is rather unfortunate and some of those families are strengthened to just continue without children. And that state of affairs is also fine if such a couple decides to continue in this way. Other childless couples decide to adopt a child to augment their familial bond and that is also fine.

Then some other variations of family units are: single-parent families; extended families; step-families or blended-families and grandparent families.

We are now talking about a family where there is a couple (husband and wife), as well as one or more children.

This is where the dynamics within the family start to change.

Now we have two or more bonds and relationships that need to be understood and taken care of.

On the one hand, there is a relationship between a husband and wife. On the other hand, there is a relationship between parents and children. Furthermore, you have a relationship that develops between children or siblings amongst one another. Different bonds and dynamics are starting to come into play here. Even between siblings, one might find stronger bonds between brothers and different ones between sisters. Then there is the bond between fathers and daughters and the bond between mothers and sons.

How to deal with all the different bonds, relationships and dynamics is an important matter. If one does not understand how it affects the other, one might find much difficulty in the familial relationship as a whole.

In this chapter, we want to highlight the main relationship that should stand above all the others in the family. That is the relationship between a husband and wife.

This relationship came first and must be held high and holy, so to speak. Husbands must love their wives and vice versa. If this is the case, it brings about a sense of safety and security within the children. The mother must not regard her relationship with all or one child as stronger than her relationship with her husband. A husband must not regard his relationship with one or more of his children as more important as the one between him and his wife. With all due respect to children, sometimes they are good at splitting their parents apart. They can exploit the strong relationship that they have with one or other parent to the detriment of the marital relationship. Let's not put the blame squarely on their shoulders. The parents are the adults and should, in a mature manner, handle the various dynamics and conflicts that arise within the family from time to time.

When one parent reprimands or discipline a child for doing something wrong and that child runs to the other parent for consolation or comfort, the other parent must rise to the occasion. They must be wise and enquire what happened and what the other parent said. This may hurt a little bit, but is the right thing to do. In this way, a situation where the child plays off one parent with the other is averted. Children should realize that it will not matter if they try to play their parents off between each other because it will not work. Their parents are united and resolute in loving and disciplining their children.

Parents should demonstrate to their children how they love each other as a couple and that that bond remains holy and strong. This must come about in their everyday lives – the way they talk to each other; the way they listen to each other; the way they support each other; the way they embrace and cuddle each other; the way they handle conflict and difficulty presented to the family from outside.

Then again, effective communication remains of utmost importance. The more parents and children communicate in a loving and open manner, the better it will be for their sound and healthy relationships.

Besides honest and open communication, it is also important that families pray together.

Parents should teach their children to pray.

Parents should show their children how to pray.

Parents should fully believe in their prayers and strong relationship with God.

Parents should allow their children to also pray out loud within the family circle. They should not laugh or belittle the children if their attempts at prayer are not on the same level as theirs.

The adage: "A family that prays together stays together" is so true.

The Colossian families are encouraged by Apostle Paul in the following passages:

> "Wives, submit to your own husbands, as is fitting in the Lord. Husbands, love your wives and do not be bitter toward them. Children, obey your parents in all things, for this is well pleasing to the Lord. Fathers, do not provoke your children, lest they become discouraged."[36]

It is without a doubt that having and looking after a family is a great responsibility – a responsibility that every family member, especially the head of the family unit, must take very seriously. We must also rule well and fairly with love and consideration within the familial relationships.

Part Three
Ruling the Environment

Chapter 6
Dominion over the environment (by Andrew Maritz)

"Do not fear, little flock, for it is your Father's good pleasure to give you the kingdom"[37]

This statement by Jesus is a reference to a place earmarked for the redeemed – the new Jerusalem, which we will explore in the concluding chapter. The souls who are found in readiness at His return and have remained steadfast in their belief and faith in the Lord Jesus Christ are promised that they will occupy and share in God's kingdom. This indeed is what all Christians and believing souls hope and yearn for.

We have visions of God ruling in this place – a place where we see Him face to face – where we will experience eternal peace, joy and love because God Himself will be All in all. It is a place of perfection as it is the abode of the perfect and wise God.

However, we can sometimes forget that the earth was a pleasing creation of God. He was happy with His work and its outcome when creating the earth and everything in it.

> "Then God saw everything that he had made, and indeed it was very good"[38]

We should also not forget that the responsibility of all life forms on this earth was handed to us from the position of the Divine and therefore it is a responsibility to take care when exercising this dominion.

A debate that is increasingly turning into contention is the topic of climate change. One does not need to be an expert in meteorology to realise that climate change is real. If there is one fight that human beings from all nationalities, creed and cultures can unite behind, it is the fight against climate change.

All of us, whilst this planet is still our home, have a vested interest in this as does God. Having lived both in Europe and in South Africa for a number of years, it is quite apparent to me how cycles and weather patterns have changed. Talking to South Africans, they quite often say: "We have not had our eight-day rain for years now" – referring to a period of rain that is continuous and lasts almost two weeks during the winter month of August.

Recently the Western Cape region, which is renowned for its wet weather, experienced its first drought for over 150 years. It is heartening to see that climate change activists in Europe are now prepared to go all the way in order to get their message across to the authorities.

All human beings across the globe have an obligation to take care of this planet. It is the one and only planet we have at this point in time and the responsibility lies with us to ensure we deal appropriately and humanely with the earth.

Unfortunately, there is not sufficient urgency from governments, businesses and the financial sectors to curb the rapid change in the earth's atmosphere as well as the dumping of waste in our oceans and rivers. The making of profit still dictates very much how and when we do things.

A recent report from Juliet Davenport, founder and CEO of Good Energy in the United Kingdom, outlines a comprehensive plan to reduce carbon emissions by 60% by 2030 and 80% by 2050. These include using wind turbine powered energy, solar and renewable electricity for our homes, businesses and vehicles.

It is encouraging that people like Juliet is forward-thinking but a niggling thought tells us it is not enough. Many organisations, companies and businesses are not doing nearly enough to counter climate change and its effects. The planet is suffering now. Do we continue at the rate we are until it breaks? I fear that when this happens it will be irreversible.

The question to those who are only driven by profit would be: How does it benefit you when you have all the money in the world but your children and generations thereafter won't have a sea or river that they can confidently use without a threat to their health and even their lives?

There is no doubt that greed, envy and covetousness are hurting the environment. Today we already have a multitude of creatures that are extinct due to trophy hunting and profiteering. White rhinos, found in Southern Africa, are viciously hunted for their horns, bringing the rhino population close to extinction. Apostle James wrote the following:

> "For where envy and self-seeking exist, confusion and every evil thing are there"[39]

These wise words underline the message:

> "A man with an evil eye hastens after riches, and does not consider that poverty will come upon him"[40]

We were given the mandate to have dominion over all life forms on the earth by God. This firstly is a divine commission. The spiritual teaching is to be responsible to our environment. This includes having dominion over our thoughts, feelings, speech and conduct. This disposition comes about by using the gifts of God's Spirit, the Holy Spirit. These gifts, already highlighted in earlier chapters, bring about the meekness that Jesus preached about in the Sermon on the Mount:

> "Blessed are the meek: for they shall inherit the earth"[41]

Jesus does not by any means deny that human beings have certain feelings and desires, but He does warn against giving them free rein. He calls for radical action against the sinfulness inherent in man. This also includes the imperative to take human dignity – which has been unconditionally conferred upon each and every individual as a creation of God – seriously. Obedience to the commandments and esteem for our neighbour protect us from adopting the wrong attitude toward possessions in general. This creates harmony and assures peace.

Politics and the financial systems that are operated have great influence over the environment and its well-being in modern times. This is not a new phenomenon. Already in Jesus' time on earth, He had many discourses with the powers that be. He refused to dine with the scribes and Pharisees as He felt they did not truly have the wellbeing of their fellow man at heart. Jesus questioned their integrity and also put them straight as to the true interpretation of the law. The law was, after all, given by God so Jesus was best qualified to profess the law.

In another incident, Jesus angrily removed the money changers and sellers from the temple. Those who were in positions to influence the quality of life and the environment positively failed to do so. Nicodemus, who was a pharisee and member of the Sanhedrin, visited Jesus and enquired about His teaching. Have we learned from this and what has changed?

Today, as in the time of Jesus, politics and finance still have great influence over the environment. If we learned anything from the 2007/8 global financial crisis and stock market crash, it's that it does not have a reset or a refresh button for when things go bad. One can reboot a computer and in fact, we as humans reset ourselves through sleep, but there is no reset button for financial markets.

The only way it resets itself is by completely crashing. We witnessed the effect of the recession which began in 2007 and the chaos and devastation it caused to many across the globe. Millions of people lost their jobs, homes and businesses which lead to broken lives. This is what happens when one takes a narrow view of things. In this case, it was solely about self-enrichment and profiteering.

The effects of the global recession are still prevalent today and dictate the quality of life or lack thereof almost 13 years later. It required the taxes of ordinary citizens through government bailouts to save the banking systems and consequently the economies of the world. The ordinary man saved the machinations of the rich and wealthy and ironically handed power back to them. New rules and regulations, put in place to govern the world of finance to prevent another catastrophe, are not nearly enough and another crash looms on the horizon.

Those who hold political power and govern today are amongst the first to admit that democracy is not without its flaws. Yet we persist with it because there is apparently no better replacement for it. In the meantime, self-enrichment, corruption and general disregard for the law continue. No wonder Jesus questioned the integrity of the lawmakers and money handlers of the time.

However, there are also positive stories. When Jesus visited the tax collector, Zacchaeus, and impacted his life for the better, the latter decided to give back the money he took from the people and decided to treat them fairly. It would be wise for governments and those in control of financial institutions to enquire into the teachings of Christ, as Nicodemus did.

The old adage that there is no alternative to our financial systems and democracy is a fallacy. The question is who or what rules the heart? Is it God or is it the ruler of this world?

Jesus gave the alternative to the rich young man when he enquired about His kingdom. He said, "Sell what you have and follow Me." Is it possible to follow the example of Jesus? To reason like Him? To speak like Him? To serve like Him? To live as He did here on earth? The answer is 'yes'. This is exactly what God, the Creator, wants from all human beings. We will do well to at least try to emulate Jesus. The dominion over living things here is already a precursor to the reign in the Thousand-Year Kingdom of Peace which we read about in the book of Revelation and in a later chapter in this book.

We could recover from the global financial crash of 2007/8 only because everyone from every background, race, creed or culture chipped in to avoid a global depression. We can also rebuild broken democracies if the collective will exist. But whatever we lose through climate change will not be recovered for future generations – it could be lost forever and what a pity that would be.

As responsible rulers and stewards over this earthly realm, we have to exercise restraint, be sober-minded, speak out and do that which is right for the preservation of the earth. One day, we will be accountable to God for this stewardship and we have to answer to the Almighty about our dominion, whether good or bad. If we cannot even rule wisely over earthly things, how can we even think of taking charge over eternal things?

Holy Communion (by Andrew Maritz)

If you were asked what you know about love – what would your answer be? How would you describe it (love)? Would you refer to the love of family – or perhaps a friend? What are the measures to love? What is the capacity of it? Where or when does it start or indeed where does it finish? Why can we not own and control it? Yet we all experience love to some degree or another. Our fondest memories are based on it. Our greatest moments are founded upon it – and still, we cannot explain it or at the best of times comprehend it.

At times, love overwhelms us with joy to the point of tears. We experience the proverbial 'lump in the throat'. Sorrows fade the same moment as peace manifests itself. Fear is forgotten and everything is perfect. We want to remain here. Surely this is home even though we cannot describe it fully or indeed understand it completely.

The content and significance of Holy Communion cannot be fully grasped in rational or even doctrinal terms. In Holy Communion, the devotion of God is experienced. Jesus Christ Himself instituted The Lord's Supper (Holy Communion). It is a sacrament which is a fundamental pillar that the Church of Christ is built on.

Holy Communion is a meal of remembrance because it, first of all, commemorates the innocent suffering and death of Jesus Christ – where God showed us to what extent He would go for us, the work of His Hand. The remembrance extends further, namely to the resurrection of the Lord and to His ascension into heaven.

It is also a meal of profession as we profess our faith, belief and trust in God. It is a visible expression and reinforcement of life with Jesus Christ. We do not just partake of Holy Communion ritually. All that we are – body, soul and spirit in unison – recognises that Jesus Christ left the glory of God to share in a life form that is beneath Him and shared our experiences – the deep hurt at losing a loved one; sorrow when we are unjustly cast away; the feeling of hunger and thirst when there is nothing to eat or drink. Christ abased Himself to our level and by doing so He changed a life that was wandering aimlessly and gave it purpose – gave it hope. Christ is the light that shines into the obscurity of darkness that separates us from our God.

In the celebration of Holy Communion, the Risen One also has fellowship with those believers who partake of the Lord's Supper worthily for their salvation. When He is near, there is no place for cares, worries and burdens, however momentarily we are relieved of them. Everything matters and nothing matters at the same time. Life stands still and continues at the same time. We experience a foretaste of the kingdom to come. When the Lord enters, our cup of joy overflows. Holy Communion purifies. It is closely associated with the remission of sin. Our resolve to resist evil and overcome our weaknesses is strengthened by it. We are constantly given the opportunity of a fresh start – a new garment. We grow into the new creation in Christ. Our hearts grow a little more. We become God-like and don't see ourselves and our problems anymore but are more concerned for those who still do not see the grace on offer.

Holy Communion frees the soul from the yoke of this world and realms beyond. Its effect will never be understood in logical terms. It was not created for the mind. It was created for the joy of life itself.

Owing to its great importance, Holy Communion is to be celebrated in reverence, faith and complete devotion to Christ. We stand in awe of His grace. We know He wants us to share in His indescribable love forever. He overcame sin and death! He resurrected to eternal life, and which he also gives to His followers.

An experience of faith during Holy Communion (By Andrew Maritz)

During my stay in Britain I often had to officiate and conduct the divine services myself. The ministers were not that many and covered long distances to the churches and halls to hold services. My family and I attended in Hitchin, about 35 kilometres from Milton Keynes where we lived. We never complained about the journey as we were always happy to see our fellow brethren when we arrived in Hitchin. Likewise, they always warmly welcomed us.

The services were held at 10 am Sunday mornings and 8 pm Wednesday evenings. Sunday morning service were usually followed with tea and cake or even some savoury snacks. My kids, Emily and Alex who were between the ages of 6 and 8, enjoyed it very much. We all enjoyed this fellowship with the congregation as we would only see each other at church.

On Sundays the little town hall would be filled but on Wednesday evenings not so because of members working late. Also traveling could be treacherous during the winter months when the road can get slippery and it becomes dangerous to drive. The result being that only a handful could attend on Wednesday evenings. It was on such a Wednesday evening that I had the most extraordinary experience.

The way we had the chairs and altar setup in the hall, meant that there was a middle walkway to the altar with the members seating either side. Towards the back of the hall the entrance from the door would lead to the middle walkway. Like so many previous divine services the sermon for the day was completed and we were leading into celebrating Holy Communion. After the standing congregation all joined in to pray the Lord's Prayer, I then followed it with the words of the absolution. It is usually followed by a short prayer of reverence before consecrating the bread and wine.

As I closed my eyes and bowed my head for the prayer before Holy Communion, I could still see everything inside the building. Everything exactly as it was. I was seeing through my mind's eye – my forehead – or spiritual eye. This was most unusual but I started the prayer anyway. While I was praying a man walked into the hall from the entrance and turned towards the altar and headed towards me down the middle walkway. I immediately felt uneasy but for the sake of the congregation I kept on praying. From the first moment I saw him I knew he was not ordinary – in fact I thought that I was seeing a ghost. By the time he reached the altar I was petrified and trembling and just wanted to finish the prayer quickly so I could open my physical eyes.

He had on a tunic which would have been the dress sense in Jesus's time here on earth. It was however no ordinary tunic. It went down to his ankles and everything about it said royalty. From the cut to the styling was regal and across the chest was covered by many squares, each one embroidered with a different pattern. It would have taken years for someone to make it. Even his sandals looked quality unlike anything I have seen before. He's hair was long curly locks that came up to his neck and he had a beard of shorter locks which was like the beards that I have seen on the old white Greek statues of prominent historical figures – but even his beard seemed unique. His whole body was white but still distinctive to the white amazing crystal-clear white of his clothing. His appearance was radiant, like when you increase the lighting on your cell phone. As the altar was ground level he came and stood right in front of it looking at me in silence.

It must have been seconds before I completed the prayer of thankfulness and opened my eyes. At the same moment he was not there anymore. I consecrated bread and wine and we all continued into celebrating the sacrament of Holy Communion.

Driving home after the divine service I could not bring myself to tell my wife Martha and the kids about my experience. Partly because I did not want to scare the kids and partly because of the conundrum in my head – I could not decide whether I had seen an angel or could I be so presumptuous to think it was the Lord Himself? This bothered me for some time. I had doubts that anyone would believe me if I told them about it. The experience was so surreal and heavenly though that I wanted it to remain so and not tell anyone. It was six months later that I only told Martha about this divine visitation.

As I carried on with normal life the memory of this event kept coming back to me every now and then. Two years had passed and on one particular day I told myself it was not an angel, but indeed it WAS the Lord. I finally convinced myself. The very same evening I went to bed and fell asleep. An hour or so into my deep sleep the same face appeared I had seen at the altar in Hitchin congregation. This time only the face appeared and I could see the rings in His eyes (pupils). I was literally stunned out of my sleep and immediately sat up in bed. It was as if Jesus could say, "finally you see!"

I have not made the same experience again during the celebration of Holy Communion. I don't have to. The Lord's promise that "where two or three gathers in My name, there I will be to bless them", is enough for me. It is Christ that makes Holy Communion special. I will always cherish this moment.

Chapter 7
Dominion over the Community (by Andrew Maritz)

There are many different communities – each different in its sociology, diversity, commonality, beliefs and even economic and historical background. It may appear daunting and an impossibility to have dominion over the community. However, Scripture reveals that there is a divine expectation from those who will be selected by God to reign and to be servants with Jesus Christ during the Thousand-Year Kingdom of Peace. Based on this, dominion over the community takes on a different dimension. It is not a rule of dictatorship or totalitarianism if you like, but more a rule of grace with emphasis on eternal peace and bliss.

According to the Oxford dictionary, 'Community' means a group of people living in the same place or having a particular characteristic in common. It is furthermore the condition of sharing or having certain attitudes and interests in common, like the sense of community that organized religion can provide. However, according to Wikipedia: "A community is a social unit (a group of living things) with commonality such as norms, religion, values, customs, or identity. Communities may share a sense of place situated in a given geographical area (e.g. a country, village, town or neighbourhood) or in virtual space through communication platforms."

Parents and individuals generally want the best for their children. They will do their utmost to navigate the children through life to success – sometimes at great sacrifice and cost to them. When things don't go as planned, fear and disappointment take over and negativity sets in. This, of course, applies to all members of society, not only Christians. How we approach and deal with what life throws at us is fundamental to the future that God promises to the community of saints in His kingdom of peace.

> "Blessed and holy is he who has part in the first resurrection. Over such the second death has no power, but they shall be priests of God and of Christ, and shall reign with Him a thousand years."[42]

Looking at the challenges we all face today, this may seem a far cry away. Jesus already warned that to follow Him would require resilience and courage – that it would sometimes feel like a lonely road to travel. However, the Holy Spirit was given to be with us and in us. The task of this wonderful Spirit is to lead us to the day of redemption, the first resurrection. God strengthens us continuously through His Spirit in word and sacrament, and boy – do we need this today!

"Durable relations that extend beyond immediate genealogical ties also define a sense of community, important to their identity, practice, and roles in social institutions such as family, home, work, government, society, or humanity at large. Although communities are usually small relative to personal social ties, 'community' may also refer to large group affiliations such as national communities, international communities, and virtual communities. The English language word 'community' comes from the Latin communitas 'community', 'public spirit' (from Latin communis, 'shared in common').

Human communities may share intent, belief, resources, preferences, needs, and risks in common, affecting the identity of the participants and their degree of cohesiveness."[43]

It is already apparent from the definition of community that it is varied and complex. In South Africa, for example, one sees many different communities based on class or finance as well as cultural similarity and even historical background.

I want to start by honouring my parents without whom I would not be the person I am today. Even though they endured poverty, I remember the struggle just to put food on the table for us – and the indignity of institutionalised segregation through apartheid in South Africa. Through challenges of accident and illness, they instilled values in us as children that are of great benefit now. A heartfelt thanks, Mom and Dad!

I have always been fascinated by world-renowned physicist, cosmologist and professor of mathematics and science, Stephen Hawking. It was, however, not his knowledge and theories of the cosmos and science that interested me. It was more how he grappled all his life with the conundrum of whether God exists or not. There was a period in his life when he was convinced that God had a hand in the creation of the universe and then in later years he backtracked and became an atheist. Amongst some of his many anecdotes, Hawking revealed: *"If you like, you can call the law of science 'God', but it wouldn't be a personal God that you would meet, and ask questions"*.

I am well aware there are different individuals that make up a community. Some would be gnostic, some agnostic. This perhaps would be for another discussion. Here we will focus on the community of the believers and the positive impact they have had and still have in society today.

Whichever community we choose to look into, there can be no doubt that moral decay has set in and taken a firm grip on many societies. In the Cape Flats, an area in Cape Town where I was born and grew up in, countless horror stories of drug abuse, gender violence, gangsterism, xenophobia, rape and murder are reported all too frequently.

The town of Nyanga has the notorious and infamous reputation of being the murder capital of South Africa. The community is up in arms over gender-based violence – in particular, violence against women and children. The abduction of children for ransom is a real fear for parents. Schools have done what they can to teach their scholars to stay in groups and be vigilant when it comes to their safety. In some crime-ridden towns, the army has been deployed to assist the police who are understaffed and, in some cases, compromised. The reality of a broken community could almost not be more vivid than this. The social injustices are exacerbated by a government who appears disconnected from a marginalised community – a truly demoralising situation. But what can we do? How do we counter this evil? By throwing money at it? Even in the affluent communities, it is fear that dictates.

Communities also bond together. If community life is threatened, they try to support one another in various ways. There are legal and illegal ways. The legal ways could include such things as supporting one another with practical and material things such as food and clothing. It happens a lot when parts of a community have suffered terrible fires or floods. The community spirit then shows itself well in such instances.

However, in instances of criminality perpetrated against members of a community, they would rally together and organise themselves to start neighbourhood watches in order to protect themselves against crime and social pathologies.

It is important that neighbourhood watches work closely with the police, otherwise, they could run the risk of becoming vigilante groups.

Other members of communities decide to start non-governmental organisations (NGOs) with the vision to uplift broken and poor communities. It has happened in many countries around the world and will continue to do so in future.

Some NGOs are faith-based and embark on a calling from God to invest strongly in certain communities to help in a natural and humanistic way and, through that, also fulfil a spiritual calling to point the way unto Jesus Christ. Christians are called to respond in such ways to help their fallen man and to bring them to God for eternal benefits. This is another profound way for children of God to exercise 'control' within certain communities. Remember, children of God have to break through hostile enemy terrain that had certain communities in spiritual bondage over many years and even centuries.

The Epistle of Paul to the Ephesians states:

> "For we do not wrestle against flesh and blood, but against principalities, against powers, against the rulers of the darkness of this age, against spiritual hosts of wickedness in the heavenly places"[44]

As much as we humans think the fight is against one another or over land and possessions for the future of our children, it goes well beyond such simplicity. We have to stave off dark spirits which want to take hold of us and for this, we need God's help. In order for us to understand, we need to return to our first love. We have to look to God. Surely love needs to rule our hearts. In the subsequent verses to the Ephesians, Paul advises to take up the whole armour of God to withstand in the evil day.

God made man with free will. It is what distinguishes us from all other creatures on the earth. By doing so, God Himself will not impose on man's free will. In turn, man cannot impose on the free will of his neighbour. Man can encourage, discourage, influence and teach others, but he cannot impose himself on others. I say this in particular to the scourge of men abusing women and children.

Whilst not even God will impose on our free will and we, therefore, cannot impose on others' free will, we can, however, make this imposition on ourselves. We can impose upon ourselves not to deal or take drugs. We can impose upon ourselves not to maim and kill. We can impose on ourselves not to sin. We can even impose upon ourselves to do good. This is how we can exercise our free will. It is worth remembering that free will is a gift from above – a divine gift.

> "And do not be conformed to this world, but be transformed by the renewing of your mind, that you may prove what is that good and acceptable and perfect will of God"[45]

The same applies to virtual communities. It is evident that self-control is lacking here. The internet, with all the platforms and applications that run on it, is regarded as the place to be today if you want success and prosperity. Many businesses would not survive without it. In fact, industries would crash without it. It has become indispensable to modern-day living. The idea of putting combinations of 0's and 1's together to form algorithms and consequently write programs for mainframe and supercomputers was, at its inception, hailed as genius. It is to date the last great invention of our time and is nearly one hundred years in the making.

As much as we laud the internet, we also have our reservations about it. The one complaint that frequently arises is the question of one's privacy. The European Union is currently the only organisation that appears to want to hold tech companies accountable for privacy bridges. It does not help that a comprehensive set of laws has not been written to stop the exploitation of people on social media by tech companies. Profit over privacy dictates. Children are exposed to content that they are nowhere near capable of processing in a mature and rational way. Parents are asked to monitor their children's activity on social media. Responsible parents do, but they cannot stop the filtering through of content every second of the day. Abuse has also become rife on social media. The lack of respect towards differing views and attacks on what people hold dear is par for the course.

I often wonder how it is that the word 'humility' has disappeared from our vocabulary. One does not even hear it on the radio or television. Humility, or humbleness, is perceived as a weakness in modern-day society. It is not in line with the 'go get spirit' of the time. Yet humbleness towards God is such an empowering characteristic. When we show our humbleness towards God in every way, He shares His power, which is infinite, with us. There is nothing more powerful than this. Humbleness, together with the understanding of its significance in the completion of God's work of salvation on the earth, brings blessing, peace and thankfulness. Jesus already alluded to it when He said the meek shall inherit the earth. He was the protagonist of humbleness. We would make this world a little better by showing humility – the sign of a big heart.

The community of believers is certainly not spared the perils, challenges and injustices of this world. Intolerance of Christian communities in some countries can be fatal. Whilst we can worship Jesus Christ freely in South Africa, it is not so easy in other countries. We think of the Coptic Christians in Egypt that are being persecuted for their beliefs. In China, Christian worship is still very much done underground. Even in Israel, the birthplace of Christianity, it is not always easy for our Christian brethren. They do amazing work in their communities and are devoted to their faith.

The believer is devoted to Christ and enquires into the will of God. They have come to know that God wants to reconcile man with Himself for good. To this end, God gave all the means through His servants and messengers and by His own Hand to accomplish His work. In Jesus Christ, the believer sees the incarnation of God in the form of man – an example for all men and women to follow.

God established the sacraments by which life with Him can be possible again. He expects Man to use the example of Jesus to attain eternal life. Jesus shows us how the conduct of his followers should be and how to react in all situations and under all conditions on the earth. Through His resurrection from death, He showed the power of God and the future for man. He returned to His kingdom and promised that He will come again and share His glory with man. God sent the Helper, the Holy Spirit, to abide with Man until Jesus' return.

The community of believers is strengthened by sharing in God's Word and the sacraments. They faithfully hold on to the promise of Jesus' return. They follow Jesus' example in prayer to God and experience His nearness through His Spirit. God allows them to have experiences with Him to strengthen their faith and resolve in times of trial.

The community of believers professes the gospel of Jesus Christ and endeavours to practise it diligently. They celebrate and partake in the sacrament of Holy Communion where they not only commemorate Christ's victory over death and sin but also strengthen their own resolve to overcome sin and take on the nature of Jesus. Together in fellowship, they praise and worship God as the omnipotent and only God and Father – the source of all love and goodness. His Son, Jesus Christ, gives grace for the perfection of the new glorified creature that man is to become. God's Spirit, The Holy Spirit, accompanies them until the return of Christ.

The community of believers trusts God implicitly. They thank Him in prayer for His love towards them. They also thank Him for His grace, blessings, goodness, mercies, gifts and protection for body, soul and spirit.

They praise, thank and worship Him even under duress and during the trials of life. They accept what God allows them to endure and know that He gives the strength to hold on to their belief and faith. The community of believers endeavours to put in practice the fruits of the Holy Spirit by showing care and compassion towards their fellow man and bearing with him irrespective of his creed, appearance or beliefs.

They also share with their neighbour that God wants to save all mankind and His help and grace are for them as well – that God's redeeming grace goes into the beyond after the natural life ends and He wants man to share in His eternal glory.

It is in all likelihood that the future community of saints will comprise of past and present faithful followers of Christ – those who countered evil with good – those who showed dominion in their communities with compassion, faith and love.

A personal and astounding experience (by Andrew Maritz)

I was in my early twenties, living in my own house in a town named Summer Greens on the Cape Flats. In the early hours one Sunday morning while still in bed sleeping, I heard a knock on the door. When I opened it, in front of me stood both my parents, tears running down their faces.

I immediately realised something was gravely wrong. Without saying a word and without even inviting them in, I immediately turned around, went straight back to my bed and pulled the covers over my head. My parents let themselves in and came to my room. As I lay down, head covered, they relayed to me the tragic incident of my brother James who had been shot five times. Not knowing how to respond, the only thing I could say back to them was, "He should have come out with me last night instead of taking off to a different party". I feared my brother was dead but my parents continued and said James was in a critical condition in Groote Schuur hospital. They had hardly finished this sentence – I was up in a flash – with a determination that to this day even surprises me.

We contacted the hospital and were told that James had been taken to theatre for emergency surgery which may take hours. There was not much the family could do other than rally around one another for support. We all got together at my sister's, Sharon's, place. Needless to say, many silent prayers were placed before God for a successful operation and to save our brother. Not many words were spoken to one another. Everyone was embroiled in their own thoughts but we all knew who the focus was on.

To break the morbid silence, I decided to put some music on. Strangely enough, it was not one of the many gospel cd's that Sharon had in her collection but rather a Miles Davis cd. The piece that resonated with all of us and that was most appropriate under the circumstances was called "Blue in Green".

I then remembered the argument I had had with James a couple of weeks prior and how I inappropriately used the Lord's Name in anger even though I knew this was against the Christian teaching. I also remembered the number 111 following me around everywhere I went. Whenever I was driving, the moment the mileage gauge ticked to 111, it would eerily draw my attention to it. This would happen when I was working on my computer as well and wherever a numbering system was in operation. The numbers 111 had a significance which I did not understand. Why would I get drawn to it at every opportunity then? James' tragic shooting only occurred on the first of November that year 1/11.

A few hours later, my parents and I decided to go to the hospital – if nothing else but just to be closer to James. It was around midday and we were waiting in the parking area. Then something happened which never happened before and to this day has not happened again. I had a complete blackout. For a while, I was in total darkness with my eyes wide open. I had no control over it whatsoever. Tears streamed from my eyes without my control. My Dad, immediately sensing my grief and thinking the worst, threw his arms up in the air and broke down weeping.

My response to the sense of my brother's enduring separation from us was immediate. I engaged God in prayer and, as I was praying, all the memories of James' life flashed through my mind in what appeared to have been seconds. In it, I saw the good things that James did. The times when we as young boys carried and placed chairs and benches for church services in our local school hall, James singing in the choir and so forth. Out of desperation, I promised God that James would do more for Him and His work should He allow James to live. The time was around ten minutes before one in the afternoon.

The hours were ticking by and still, we were waiting for any news on the operation. Only in the early evening did we get the news that James was out of theatre and we could see him. When we saw him, his eyes were shut. Not knowing what to say, I just spoke the first thing that came to mind and said, "So you went to battle without me then, hey?" James, hearing my voice, immediately opened his eyes.

Upon speaking with the surgeons who came to check up on James, they confirmed that it had been touch and go and they had nearly lost him during surgery. I knew the time this occurred. Somehow James and I never really spoke about the incident much. I always assumed it was because of the events leading up to it. Years later, whilst visiting him socially, the topic surfaced for some reason. I told James all that had happened while he was in hospital and how I had desperately pleaded with God to spare his life.

James, in turn, shared his experience during his surgery. He said that at some point he was floating away from earth to a place he did not know but, while he kept moving, he saw people with their arms and hands stretching towards him. The sense he had was that of misery and unpleasantness. He was then jerked back with a force of gravity and suddenly found himself staring the surgeons in the face, then promptly fading again. This was most likely the time they were fighting to keep him alive and sedating him again.

I have learned so much out of this one experience. From a personal point of view, I decided then never to use the Lord's Name for negative reasons ever again. Whether it had anything to do with the incident, I do not even want to know. I just know that using the Lord's Name can have devastating effects when used for anything other than good. God had wanted to hear my voice to undo the curse. I had to plead with Him to save my brother.

James was consequently ordained into the deacon ministry a couple of years later. I breathed a sigh of relief. God allowed me to be freed from my desperate promise to Him. James was now doing more for the furtherance of God's work. Soon thereafter, he was ordained into the priestly ministry and is still active today. Also, after the incident, the number 111 did not follow me around anymore. Perhaps I'm just not afraid anymore.

Chapter 8
Dominion within our Mission (by Andrew Maritz)

We all want to have a great childhood – filled with loving parents and wonderful gifts – the freedom to play and have fun and eat all our favourite foods – go to bed only when we feel like it and, if we can skip school, all the better.

We also want a great time in our teenage and young adult years. To be the popular one at school would be nice. To have one's own car would be awesome and to have that cute boy or girl on one's arm as one's boyfriend or girlfriend would just be super cool and would do wonders for one's image. We might travel the world; make new experiences – our own personal experiences; have an adventure.

We want to fall in love with someone special and get married – maybe have children of our own – maybe not have children and just be a family of husband and wife; be happy; have an important job where the world recognises our achievements or maybe just run our own business; be successful; be rich or even just comfortable would do. We want to provide for our children and be content in our latter years and at the end, die peacefully in our sleep, having had a full and happy life.

If only I could block out all the negative news on television – that would be great; to see my beloved Tottenham Hotspur Football Club win the league in my lifetime. Now that would be the cherry on the cake. That golden cockerel is already flying in my mind's eye instead of just sitting proudly on the stadium's roof.

We all have our dreams and desires. It is in our make-up. We are complex and fascinating beings – able to grasp the abstract, able to reason, able to imagine things, able to be inventive and create things. Human beings are the crown of God's creation here on earth. Human beings are created in the image of God. The fact that man has been created in the image of God means that he has been given an exceptional position within the visible creation: he is the one whom God loves and to whom God speaks.

God made man:

> "a little lower than the angels"[46]

and set him up as ruler over the earth. Having been created in the image of God, it is up to human beings to treat creation with wisdom and handle it responsibly.

Why then do we sell ourselves short when the offer of eternal fellowship with God is rejected out of hand? Should we not be investing time, energy and charity to accomplish this most glorious gift – eternal fellowship with The God of gods? The offer of a new heaven and earth is there for all mankind – where true peace can be had – where there will be no toil and strife anymore.

However long the first humans lived in close proximity to God did not change the Father when they sinned. Instead of rejecting them completely, He promised to send One to counter the evil that deceived both Adam and Eve.

Salvation history has given us some great examples through the ages of men and women who were given a seemingly impossible task to perform. Noah was charged to build the ark to protect people from the devastation of the flood to come. Moses was given the task to free his tribe from slavery and the Egyptian empire. Abraham was commanded to leave his country and everything he knew and was comfortable with, at the ripe old age of seventy-five, in order to find a new place for God's people. Ruth left her own country because of her friendship with Naomi. David was anointed as King of Israel at the tender age of fifteen. There was also Mary who raised a young Jesus and many more.

All were ordinary human beings who, inspired by God and with the help of the Holy Spirit, contributed towards God's plan of salvation, their belief and trust in God culminating in the incarnation of God Himself in the person of Jesus Christ. God Himself took on the mission to save mankind from the evil one and from themselves.

In Christ, God gave the ultimate example for human beings to emulate. In Him, we now can have the protection from all elements – natural and spiritual. In Christ, we can be freed from the yoke of evil and sin to face God in righteousness; to be His friend and to ascend from earthly to heavenly places; to experience a future of God's rule and love. It is in truth overwhelming – but this is God.

The self-abasement of God in the Man Jesus had far-reaching implications for all humans of the past, present and future. Christ Himself now confronted the devil – something we humans struggle with. Not only did He stand up to the devil but did so in human form. He pointed to the Scriptures and to the power of God the Father and His legion of angels when tempted by the devil. In essence, Christ helped us mere mortals with this fight against the devil and evil powers. He proved to us that evil does not have a lasting hold over mankind and it is within us to resist him.

Jesus' mission was to free us from the bondage of sin and thus we can emerge as new creatures in soul and spirit. This new conscience is to drive our minds and bodies. He established the forgiveness of sins to transform us and enable us to overcome our weaknesses. Whenever we celebrate Holy Communion, we can be strengthened in His ways. With His crucifixion, Jesus showed that we also need to be committed to the very end to our God without hurting others.

He also showed us an example in prayer, in serving God and how we are to treat one another as human beings. A new covenant was now established between God the Creator and the crown of His earthly creation, mankind. The portal of grace was opened by which mortal man can take on immortality. Jesus' resurrection shows the way for us:

> "I am the way, the truth and life. No one comes to the Father except through Me."[47]

The work, however, did not stop with Christ's return to His glory. God gave us the Comforter and Helper to abide with us as well as in us – The Holy Spirit. God is well aware that the fight against the evil one will continue until His kingdom of peace is established. It is for this reason that Christ promised His disciples God's Spirit.

> "And I will pray the Father, and He will give you another Helper, that He may abide with you forever – the Spirit of truth, whom the world cannot receive, because it neither sees Him nor knows Him; but you know Him, for he dwells with you and will be in you."[48]

Jesus Christ certainly fulfilled his mission here on earth with power and majesty yet showing that no one is greater than God. He humbled Himself to the point of physical death. He established His Church and opened the portals of grace for mankind. He opened access to God in a special way whereby we can have a relationship with God. The expectation from above is that we follow the example set by the Lord. What a responsibility. How do we do this?

We do not have the capacity to defeat evil ourselves. The good news is that we do not have to. The power of God through Christ and the Holy Spirit has already overcome on our behalf in this regard. Christ has already defeated the devil's greatest selling point – that life ends at natural death. More so, the gospel even alludes to the second death – the separation between God and the immortal soul which the evil one has no power over. God is still the Master of His domain and as such the universe and everything in it.

In essence, our mission is God's mission. We are to continue in God's ways. The way to eternal fellowship with God has already been established by God Himself. The Church of Christ is also established. The sacraments have been implemented by Christ. God also abides with us in Spirit. We have been given the Scriptures, the Gospel of Jesus Christ, as a guide to our lives and the commandments to live justly. We are well endowed to execute this mission. Let us rule in this domain.

There is no doubt that it will be challenging but God's reward and vision for mankind far surpass the pain and discomfort we may have to endure. Our mission is not to convince anyone about God and His existence. Instead, our mission is to show God in our own lives. We ought to do the things that draw Him to us. These are to worthily partake of His sacraments, follow His teachings and be with Him when Christ returns at the rapture of the Church.

At the return of Christ, the scope of everything we know here on earth will change but God's grace towards mankind will continue. The marriage of the saved with Christ in heaven will coincide with the period of tribulation on earth. Christ will, however, return with the saints to establish His kingdom of peace.

Looking at the world today, a different picture emerges. It is an image of a materialistic place where everyone is only concerned about self and the need for self-gratification. Instead of love, fear drives many. Success is measured by how much material wealth we have. Morals or indeed values are not considered in the pursuit for riches or even fame. Even the wellbeing of the planet – the only one we can live on – is secondary. Countries are ravaged by war and famine and yet there appears no end to the negative trajectory of economies across the globe. The fear of lawlessness and chaos is palpable and, more worryingly, visible. Do we ever need a Saviour now! Do we ever need a higher Love!

We have an anchor though – One whom we can always look to when the waters get too choppy. He has provided us with all the tools to continue in His way. As we strive to be in one mind with God, we will also increase in strength. God will not allow His own to carry more than they can bear.

Our mission should be to reach out to all people, teaching them the gospel of Jesus Christ and baptising them with water and the Holy Spirit – providing soul care and cultivating a warm fellowship in which everyone experiences the love of God and the joy of serving Him and others.

Throughout the history of the Church of Jesus Christ, many church denominations, groupings and foundations have endeavoured to 'missionize' the world. One such missionary endeavour is the three journeys that Apostle Paul undertook to some parts of Asia Minor and further abroad.

This gives power and life to the "Great Commission" that Jesus gave His followers – that we must go out to the four corners of the world to bring the testimony of His gospel to all nations. Through many centuries, the flow and direction were outwards from the Middle East and Europe to the Third World countries. However, it seems that now there could be a reverse happening from certain parts of the Third World (like Africa and Asia) toward European countries. This is evident owing to the fact that true and deep-felt Christianity has weakened considerably in western countries in favour of the so-called modernisation and materialism.

One global missionary foundation that does great but unassuming work is that of Open Doors. They have a mission to serve the persecuted Church which is that part of the Church of Christ where believers are severely persecuted for their Christian faith – in countries where such persecution is not only allowed to take place but actively encouraged by those governments and laws. Every year, Open Doors publish a 'Worldwide Watch List' that depicts the 50 countries where it is most difficult to be a Christian as a result of persecution. We have to support our persecuted brethren through prayers and resources, as they form part of us as the bigger Church.

Part Four
Ruling in Moneymaking Settings

Chapter 9
Dominion within the work setting

Work?

What is it and why do we have to do it?

According to the Oxford dictionary, the word 'work' can be understood in two ways: as a noun, as well as a verb.

As a noun:

1. activity involving mental or physical effort done in order to achieve a purpose or result;
2. a task or tasks to be undertaken.

As a verb:

1. be engaged in physical or mental activity in order to achieve a result; do work;
2. (of a machine or system) function, especially properly or effectively.
E.g. "his phone doesn't properly work unless he goes to a high point".

But why do we as human beings have to work and who instructed us to do it?

Let's turn to Holy Scripture.

Firstly, God worked by creating heaven and earth and everything in it (including humans). He worked for six days before He took a full day of rest.

Then He blessed man and said:

> "Be fruitful and multiply; fill the earth and subdue it; have dominion over the fish of the sea, over the birds of the air, and over every living thing that moves on the earth. And God said, 'See, I have given you every herb that yields seed which is on the face of all the earth, and every tree whose fruit yields seed; to you it shall be for food. Also, to every beast of the earth, to every bird of the air, and to everything that creeps on the earth, in which there is life, I have given every green herb for food'; and it was so. Then God saw everything that He had made, and indeed it was very good."[49]

This was all good and fine while Man and everything else was perfect and good. However, after the 'fall' of man where SIN entered the scene, things changed dramatically.

God's curse:

> "Cursed is the ground for your sake; In toil you shall eat of it all the days of your life. Both thorns and thistles it shall bring forth for you, and you shall eat the herb of the field. In the sweat of your face you shall eat bread till you return to the ground, for out of it you were taken; for dust you are, and to dust you shall return."[50]

Thus, initially, the mandate to work was something beautiful and pleasant. However, after the 'fall', a curse was attached to it. To work was no longer just an enjoyable engagement – it was so much harder! It went hand in hand with much toil and sweat. But Man had to do it because, without it, he would go hungry and die. Man had to work the field and animals in order to 'put bread on the table' so to speak, in order to sustain himself, as well as his family.

Thus, Man was destined to work and to continue to work. He had to do it, on the one hand, to sustain himself as well as his family. But on the other hand, he had to work to have dominion over the earth. The initial mandate God had given him did not fall away with sin. He still had to have control over his environment, albeit so much more difficult to do.

Man gained control over the animals (especially the cattle) to work for them. Just think of the donkeys or cows that man used to pull yokes to plough the fields and carry heavy loads for him.

Over time, man discovered that he could kill some animals for meat to eat and could obtain milk to drink from cows and goats.

Man discovered that he could also use certain types of earth, such as clay, to build houses and buildings to live and work in.

We know that for many centuries human beings lived essentially from the produce of the earth through those things that he could plant and harvest on the farms. This state of affairs continued until human beings discovered the innovation of the wheel. The wheel assisted greatly and made the life of man slightly easier. A wheel is a circular object that revolves on an axle and is fixed below a vehicle or other object to enable it to move easily over the ground.

With this invention, other inventions and innovations soon followed that made life even easier for man. It took some of the load off his shoulders, pun intended.

These discoveries and innovations were just proof that man was made in God's image. God is the Creator. Man is also a creator in a lesser form. God instilled in man the ability to be creative and innovative. He gave man the authority to have dominion over the earth and to subdue it.

This ability of man enabled him to think of new ideas and innovations and employ the skills of his hands and the use of animals and machinery to do more and greater things. Without these, he would not be in a position to do them. Think about the carts or wagons that were pulled by using horses or other animals. This led further to the discovery of machinery. Thus, the shift began to move away from human beings being solely dependent on produce from fields or farms to doing work slightly removed therefrom into towns and cities. There many more people could be employed to produce single items on a grand scale to be sold to other companies that needed them.

These ideas and innovations, therefore, led to the first industrial revolution.

"The industrial revolution was the transition to new manufacturing processes in Europe and the United States, in the period from about 1760 to sometime between 1820 and 1840. Agricultural societies became more industrialized and urban. The transcontinental railroad, the cotton gin, electricity and other inventions permanently changed society. There was the Spinning Jenny which was a spinning engine invented in 1764 by James Hargreaves. Thereafter came the steam engines and locomotives, as well as the steam engines of large ships (steamboats with power to travel upstream); the diesel engine; the aeroplane; the telegraph communications; dynamite to assist with mining operations; the photograph; the typewriter, and so forth.

This was a time when the manufacturing of goods moved from small shops and homes to large factories. This shift brought about changes in culture as people moved from rural areas to big cities in order to work.

Thereafter came the Second Industrial Revolution, which was also known as the Technological Revolution. This ushered in a phase of rapid industrialization from the late 19th century into the early 20th century. Advancements in manufacturing and production technology enabled the widespread adoption of technological systems such as telegraph and railroad networks, gas and water supply, and sewage systems, which had earlier been concentrated to a few select cities. New systems such as electrical power and telephones were introduced, as well as the electrification of the production line, and ended at the beginning of World War 1.

The Third Industrial Revolution is also known as the Digital Revolution. Beginning in the 1950s, the third industrial revolution brought semiconductors, mainframe computing, personal computing, and the Internet – the digital revolution. Things that used to be analogue moved to digital technologies, like an old television with an antenna (analogue). Electronic and information technology began to automate production and take supply chains global.

The Fourth Industrial Revolution: Now!

Each of the first three industrial revolutions represented profound change. Life went from being all about the farm to all about the factory, and people moved from the country into town with the introduction of mechanical production. Most recently, once again the digital revolution altered nearly every industry, transforming how people live, work and communicate.

Maybe we don't have flying cars yet, but we've got robots. Plus, there is genetic sequencing and editing, artificial intelligence, miniaturized sensors and 3D printing, to name a few.

Some countries are still very stuck in the third industrial revolution, with elements of the fourth industrial revolution emerging.

However, this is the way of the world now and is going to impact how people view work into the future."[51]

It does not really matter how technologies change and how they impact our work environments. The important issues are the underlying values, ethics and morals that underpin our work life.

What was important even before the first industrial revolution started, and remained important throughout the subsequent industrial revolutions, WILL remain important in the fourth and even fifth industrial revolutions. That entails the value systems – in other words, those things that make a human being a human being – those things that ensure we deal respectfully and graciously with one another – those values which can be regarded as human values and dignity remains important.

Here I am not even talking about godly values, ethics and morals that a child of God should display.

No matter what the work entails, the people doing it should engage with one another with respect. This respect involves those who you work with – your colleagues at the office or factory – and also those you deal with outside your workplace, i.e. your clients or customers.

Every worthwhile organisation espouses to uphold a certain vision, mission as well as values. Every worker employed at such an organisation should agree to uphold those things, otherwise, they should not be working there.

Children of God should go even further, as we are kept to a higher standard. Values such as integrity, honesty, caring, accountability, responsiveness, diligence, respect, and honour should come almost naturally to a child of God. Any business owner or senior manager would be proud to have such a worker in their employ.

And oh, just to take it a bit further: children of God should not gossip, steal, lie or try to pull their seniors or colleagues down by backbiting or any other evil schemes. On the contrary, we should work hard and earn from an honest day's work.

To take it another step further, children of God should also pray every day for the success of their organisations, as well as the wellbeing of their colleagues.

We should be thankful if we do have jobs. There are so many people who are healthy and fit but cannot find gainful employment. Let us look after the jobs we do have and bring about a positive atmosphere when we are at work. Remember we are God's representatives at our workplaces. That does not mean that we have to walk around with the Bible under our arms and verbally testify to all our colleagues about God's kingdom. But it does mean that we live our lives, even at work, as true children of God. Through the way we conduct ourselves at work, our colleagues and managers will think twice and wonder what makes us tick. When the opportunity presents itself, we can tell them who we are and whom we represent.

We will thus cherish the fact that God has given us healthy bodies and minds with skills and abilities to work in organisations that are not necessarily Christian in their composition. However, God has deemed it fit that we should be placed there to shine for Him. Through our diligent and trustworthy work ethics, many will marvel at how we carry ourselves and that might be the first step to their also becoming children of God.

God bless and prosper those organisations just merely for the fact that we are employed there.

For those who are fortunate to be working in Christian organisations, you should be happy and blessed to further the work of the kingdom of God in an almost unfettered manner.

An important godly principle, when it comes to seeking God's favour in our lives, especially in our finances, is to bring our tithes (one 10th) of our income into God's house. This is expected by God as described in Malachi 3:8-12. We are not to rob God, but to offer unto Him. Our offerings include many things: our prayers, time, sacrifice, fasting, support in ministry, giving to others less fortunate, investing in worthwhile and noble causes, and as God shows us, but also in our tithes. Through doing this, God WILL open the windows of heaven and pour out a rich blessing upon us. God will also rebuke the devourer and chase him away from us and our properties!

These are some of the ways we should use in order to exercise control within our work settings!

Chapter 10
Dominion within business and investments

Some people just have the ability and flair to run a successful business. Others don't – full stop!

For those who have been running their own businesses for a few years, you can testify that it didn't come so easily. You know what it takes. You can recall the many restless nights sweating over whether your business would succeed or not.

Running a successful business takes guts, sweat and tears – and it takes much more than that. It also requires the right mentality and frame of mind; diligence and hard work; discipline; the right idea that you believe in; the right setting and circumstances; and a lot of good fortune!

"From your business type to your business model to your physical location, there are so many variables it's not easy to come up with a list that will work "exactly so" for everybody. The key, regardless of what type of business you're starting, is to be flexible!

1) Find A Good Business Idea

A good business idea isn't just one that turns a profit. It's one that's a good fit for you personally, for your target market, and for your location. Hopefully, you're going to be in business for a long time, so pick something you love.

2) Choose The Type Of Business You Want To Start

A traditional business isn't right for everyone. If you want to hit the ground running with a tried-and-tested business model, a franchise may be a better fit for you, or if you like the idea of doing good at the same time, why not a non-profit, or a social enterprise?

3) Do Your Market Research

One of the best ways to figure out whether or not you've hit upon a good idea is to get out and start talking to real people—do they really want a fancy Basque restaurant in their neighbourhood or is another doughnut shop going to be more to their taste?

4) Test Your Business Idea

How do you really know you've hit upon a good idea? We use the lean planning methodology to figure this out. Of course, you may also want to get out and talk to real people about what they want and whether or not your product or service solves that need.

5) Write Your Business Plan

While you don't need a 40-page business plan in order to get your business up and running, if you're seeking funding, banks and investors may ask for one.

6) Brand Your Business

A strong brand is the key to customer loyalty and higher sales. Now that you know a bit more about your target audience, you've got the opportunity through your brand – to grab their attention.

7) Make It Legal

Before you can open shop and comfortably start doing business, you've got to make sure you've checked all the necessary boxes. You are going to have to do some things 'by the book'.

8) Get Financed

While not every start-up needs outside funding, most businesses do require some help, at least at the beginning. If you've worked through your business plan and have a sound handle on your financials, pitching for funding should be a breeze.

9) Market And Launch Your Business

It's time to start getting people hyped up about your opening day. This is your opportunity to get things going with a bang!"[52]

This chapter is not about the 'how' to start or maintain good business, although some good advice would not go amiss. However, it is more about how to conduct yourself if you do have a business and have to operate in a particular market or field. In other words, it's more about how one should rule in this sphere as a child of God.

Can we look at Scripture to guide us somehow? Oh yes, by all means!

Let us take a look at Abraham when he got word that Lot was taken captive by a combination of four kings. They also took all the goods of Sodom and Gomorrah and all their provisions. Immediately, Abraham took his men in pursuit of those kings and overcame them. He brought Lot back and also all the goods that were captured. The king of Sodom wanted Abraham to take the goods for himself but Abraham refused by saying:

> "I will take nothing, from a thread to a sandal strap, and that I will not take anything that is yours, lest you should say, 'I have made Abram rich'."[53]

Although Abraham could have taken those things, which he had certainly earned, he refused to take them out of generosity and goodwill. And we all know how God eventually blessed Abraham. He was indeed a very rich man in those days. God not only blessed him materially but also stretching forward in time for future generations to come.

Let us also take a look at his grandson, Jacob.

Jacob worked for his father-in-law, Laban. By agreement, it would have been for 7 years in order to marry the daughter of Laban, Rachel. However, Laban deceived Jacob by letting him first get married to his eldest daughter, Leah. He then forced Jacob to work for him another 7 years in order to eventually get married to Rachel.

After this, Laban wanted Jacob to continue to stay with him:

> "For I have learned by experience that the Lord has blessed me for your sake."[54]

However, this did not sit well with Jacob, who wanted to go on to do his own thing. Then Laban asked Jacob what he should give him. Jacob answered:

> "You shall not give me anything. If you will do this thing for me, I will again feed and keep your flocks: Let me pass through all your flocks today, removing from there all the speckled and spotted sheep, and all the brown ones among the lambs, and the spotted and speckled among the goats: and these shall be my wages."[55]

The story of Jacob going it alone in business goes further like this:

> "Thus, the man (Jacob) became exceedingly prosperous, and had large flocks, female and male servants, and camels and donkeys."[56]

We can see from these two examples that both Abraham and his grandson, Jacob, refused to take things from their contemporaries that they thought were not meant for them. They wanted God to bless them instead.

It can be a very tough and mean place to be in a business where you and your company have to make a living by selling your products or services. Many business owners today (and indeed over many past years) have done things underhandedly in order to make a quick buck.

All sorts of shortcuts are taken. The business world can be very vicious and cut-throat. Many will not even flinch when they undercut another company to get the business they want. They can be dishonest and deceitful at any time.

These dishonourable and unchristian values and principles should not be what defines a true child of God – even in the harsh business world.

I know of many business owners that would start the day of business with a prayer. They pray for their businesses, themselves and their employees. They seek God's blessing and guidance to take them through the day. They bring their offerings to God in order to thank Him but also to seek more blessing.

Other businesses respect such companies because of their values and principles and good business ethics.

If a business owner conducts his (or her) business in this godly fashion, it is also a testimony of their trust and belief in the Almighty God. Through their conduct, it could also influence their business partners and workforce to walk with God.

God's children also have many investments.

Investments include, but are not limited to, such things as savings accounts; unit trusts; stokvels; investments in the stock markets of various countries; investments in properties and timeshare; investments in cryptocurrencies; investments in paintings or other valuables; pension funds; life insurance and so on.

Some investments are good and relatively safe. Others are very risky and fluid. Some people get very rich from sensible and timely investments while others are not so fortunate.

Even here with regard to our investments, God's children are called to be wise, but also to uphold certain standards and ethics. We should pray over all our investments and ask that God also protects them for our benefit.

"We should protect and look after that which God has given us through grace. It will grieve God, as the Giver of all good gifts, if He sees that we are squandering, neglecting, and demeaning those things that He indeed has provided for us. Remember the parable of Jesus about the talents, and how the one buried his one talent thinking that his master was an austere man!

We should not only look after what He has given us but should also strive to multiply and increase it. That is the wisdom that our Lord expects of us. Obviously, in referring to the increasing of our natural gifts, we should guard against being taken over by a spirit of greed and ambition that undermine others.

We pray for God's protection over all our belongings. This protection should even extend to and cover all assets belonging to our children and grandchildren. If perhaps we have lost anything in the past through any reason, we pray that God repays (restores) us for the years that the locusts have eaten away at those things that belong to us. Remember what happened to our friend, Job from the Old Testament. He lost everything at one point, but God gave him back much more than what he lost at the end.

We must not be afraid to mention any particular aspect of our belongings that seems under threat. We are to call on God to send special angels to fight for us in those particular areas."[57]

May God grant us wisdom, strength and grace to look after our investments and possessions. May He further help to protect them, but also to grant favour to increase it. We pull the blessing of God which He has given to Abraham and his seed upon us through faith in Jesus Christ. Through Jesus, we gain access to the rich blessing of Abraham.

Part Five
Ruling In The New Jerusalem

Chapter 11
Dominion and responsibility in the Kingdom of God

"The Lord has established His throne in heaven, and His kingdom rules over all. Bless the Lord, you His angels, which excel in strength, who do His word. Bless the Lord, you His hosts, you ministers of His, who do His pleasure. Bless the Lord, all His works, in all places of His dominion."[58]

The New Jerusalem of God's everlasting Kingdom will be (is) awesome.

We are not there yet.

Yet we are there already (in some strange way of putting it).

The Psalmist also said:

> "Your kingdom is an everlasting Kingdom. And Your dominion endures throughout all generations."[59]

Stay with me on this thought.

I fully believe the Bible where Apostle Paul, through the Holy Spirit, says that we as God's children were chosen by God before the foundation of the world was laid. Consider:

> "Blessed be the God and Father of our Lord Jesus Christ, who has blessed us with every spiritual blessing in the heavenly places in Christ, just as *He chose us in Him before the foundation of the world,* that we should be holy and without blame before Him in love, having predestined us to adoption as sons by Jesus Christ to Himself, according to the good pleasure of His will, to the praise of the glory of His grace, by which He made us accepted in the Beloved"[60] [Emphasis added].

Now, this is very significant.

If we truly believe that God has chosen us as His children before the foundations of the world, then it just opens up further revelations.

God could only have chosen us if we existed.

So, **God called us into existence before the foundations of the world** and kept us somewhere safe in abeyance by His Power. He then allowed us as His children to enter into this physical world that He created, after He created us, and put us into our physical places on earth at the right times of our births through His power. Time and space are rendered irrelevant through faith! God stands way above time and space. God can easily suspend or collapse time by His choosing. With God, human time is irrelevant, albeit important to us. God has regard and respect for human time. Remember, human beings designed, developed and calculated time to make some sense of their existence and to order their living. They made calendars and clocks. But although our human time was designed and calculated by humans, it was allowed by God. He certainly gave humans the ideas, intelligence and abilities to make sense of earthly time.

Albert Einstein's theory of special relativity says that time slows down or speeds up depending on how fast you move relative to something else.

As a physicist, Einstein had many discoveries, but he is perhaps best known for his theory of relativity and the equation E=MC2, which foreshadowed the development of atomic power and the atomic bomb. He received the 1921 Nobel Prize in Physics "for his services to theoretical physics, and especially for his discovery of the law of the photoelectric effect", a pivotal step in the development of quantum theory. Some principles that he pioneered:

Theory of special relativity: Einstein showed that physical laws are identical for all observers, as long as they are not under acceleration. However, the speed of light in a vacuum is always the same, no matter at what speed the observer is travelling. This work led to his realization that space and time are linked to what we now call space-time. So, an event seen by one observer may also be seen at a different time by another observer.

Theory of general relativity: This was a reformulation of the law of gravity. In the 1600s, Newton formulated three laws of motion, among them, outlining how gravity works between two bodies. The force between them depends on how massive each object is, and how far apart the objects are. Einstein determined that when thinking about space-time, a massive object causes a distortion in space-time (like putting a heavy ball on a trampoline). Gravity is exerted when other objects fall into the "well" created by the distortion in space-time, like a marble rolling towards the large ball. General relativity passed a recent major test in 2019 in an experiment involving a supermassive black hole at the centre of the Milky Way.[61]

However, God's time is not our time. Apostle Peter said:

> "But, beloved, be not ignorant of this one thing, that one day is with the Lord as a thousand years, and a thousand years as one day."[62]

Remember, human beings designed and calculated time. They made calendars and clocks. But although our human time was designed and calculated by humans, it was allowed by God. He certainly gave humans the ideas, intelligence and abilities to make sense of earthly time. Human beings need that concept and calculation of time to make sense of the world in which we live. It helps us in our planning, scheduling, projecting, developing, business, science, order and predictability. It provides some form of security we can trust regarding the calculation of time forward and backwards, etc.

I am fascinated by a poem Helen Steiner-Rice put together about 'time':

"No time, you say?
You have no time for what you cannot
see? No time to think, no time to pray,
no opportunity? For feeding on the bread
of life by study and by prayer, for this
most precious of all, you have 'no time'
to spare.
And yet, how many moments of your
time is spent on things of no importance:
smoking, viewing, pleasure, leisure, idle
gossiping.
Yes, you seem to find time for all other things.
It's not the time you lack, although you
live at speed.
There's always time to give to God. We
all so deeply need the wisdom and the
peace bestowed when we on Him
believe.
So, make time for this, while there is still
time to ask and to receive!"[63]

Makes you think, doesn't it?

God also loved us then. It is a love that we will never be able to
comprehend – for all eternity. This love is undeserved grace that
He afforded us to become His children. This is predestination in
action. We did not contribute anything to deserve it.

Just as God chose us way back then and only allowed us to enter
this world at the right (appointed) time according to His will,
likewise He can also justify and perfect us through the Blood of
His Son. To take it a bit further, God can also create the New
Jerusalem for His eternal Kingdom and keep it in abeyance
somewhere in heaven by His power. Then He can also deposit
us into the New Jerusalem at the right time. Lastly, He can then
also deposit us all (as the children of God will also be settled into
the New Jerusalem on the new earth, descended from heaven)

to live there – with the New Jerusalem as its eternal citizens in the New Earth, as Apostle John saw in a vision.

In another sense, the New Jerusalem is also the Bride of Christ!

Note the vision of Apostle John that the angel showed him:

> "Come, I will show you the bride, the Lamb's wife. And he carried me away in the Spirit to a great and high mountain, and showed me the great city, the holy Jerusalem, descending out of heaven from God, having the glory of God."[64]

At the current moment in time, the Bride of Christ is actually the Church of Christ – but not yet fully perfected.

The Church of Christ, as the Body of Christ, must still go through its final stages of becoming fully united in love. At the moment, the Church of Jesus Christ is still a bit divided on earth in and amongst itself. The Church of Christ comprises denominations and groupings across different churches and countries on earth, as well as the other side in heaven.

Thus, the Church of Christ stretches back in time, as well as forward in time. I am confident that the part of the Church of Christ that is in heaven already achieved oneness and unity. And the heavenly part of the Church of Christ intercedes and prays constantly that God will help the earthly part of the Church to also overcome their differences and become one. It is only the part of the Church of Christ that is still on this sinful earth that needs to find true unity. This will also be achieved at the right time. Jesus is standing in the midst of the seven lampstands, as described in Revelation 1:13. The lampstands represent the seven churches in Asia – but I daresay, more importantly, it also represents His Church – meaning Jesus is standing and moving in between and through His Church across the world (as well as the part of His Church in heaven).

However, I am confident that Jesus Christ, as the Head of His Church, is currently doing everything in His power to bring about true unity and love. True unity of the Church of Jesus Christ is something that the devil hates. The devil and his scoundrels are doing their utmost to keep the Church of Jesus Christ divided and to fight amongst themselves. As long as individual members of the Church of Jesus Christ (meaning different church denominations, groups and sects) are trying to exclude one another to claim doctrinal superiority, the devil will succeed in his diabolical work. But, rest assured, Jesus also knows this and is busy bringing about true unity within His Church.

Scripture attests to the fact that there will be various stages of development in time and history that will first take place before God's people will settle in New Jerusalem.

In no particular order of importance, some of the main future events that are recorded in Scripture will, amongst others, include:

- Final signs of the times and the end of the age on earth (refer to Luke 21);
- Jesus will appear on a cloud to fetch His children (the First Resurrection and Rapture);
- The Wedding Feast in heaven will take place;
- Great tribulation on earth while the Wedding Feast is taking place;
- Jesus and His bride will fight and conquer the devil, binding him for a thousand years;
- During this millennium of peace, Jesus and His own will rule undisturbed on this old earth;
- After this millennium of peace, the devil will be set free and make war against Jesus and His own;

- God, Himself, will intervene and the devil will be cast in the lake of fire and brimstone together with the beast and false prophet where they will be tormented forever;
- Thereafter, the Great White Throne (Last) Judgement will take place where Death and Hades, as well as all those not found written in the Book of Life, will also be cast into the lake of fire;
- Then the new heaven and new earth will be created and the New Jerusalem will appear and descend onto the New Earth;
- God's people will settle on the New Earth forever in glory. They will rule with Jesus in their new capacities in the roles that He will assign to them.

This will be (is) our eternal future.

It is designed and planned by our Sovereign God and WILL happen according to His Word. We just have to do our best to align our lives according to God's Word and will. And in the final analysis, we also cannot do it on our own. We all need God's help and grace.

Let us look at the word 'sovereign' and what it means:

"If you were to look up the word 'sovereign' in the dictionary, you would find words and phrases like 'superior,' 'greatest,' 'supreme in power and authority,' 'ruler,' and 'independent of all others' in its definition. But the way I like to explain God's sovereignty best is simply to say, 'God is in control.'

Biblical Definition and Context of 'Sovereign':

There is absolutely nothing that happens in the universe that is outside of God's influence and authority. As King of kings and Lord of lords, God has no limitations. Consider just a few of the claims the Bible makes about God:

- God is above all things and before all things. He is the Alpha and the Omega, the Beginning and the End. He is immortal, and He is present everywhere so that everyone can know Him (Revelation 21:6).
- God created all things and holds all things together, both in heaven and on earth, both visible and invisible (Colossians 1:16).
- God knows all things past, present, and future. There is no limit to His knowledge, for God knows everything completely before it even happens (Romans 11:33).
- God can do all things and accomplish all things. Nothing is too difficult for Him, and He orchestrates and determines everything that is going to happen in your life, in my life, in America, and throughout the world. Whatever He wants to do in the universe, He does, for nothing is impossible with Him (Jeremiah 32:17).
- God is in control of all things and rules over all things. He has power and authority over nature, earthly kings, history, angels, and demons. Even Satan himself has to ask God's permission before he can act (Psalm 103:19).

That's what being sovereign means. It means being the ultimate source of all power, authority, and everything that exists. Only God can make those claims; therefore, it's God's sovereignty that makes Him superior to all other gods and makes Him, and Him alone, worthy of worship.'[65]

This means that God is in control and rules the universe, earth, heavens and everything that exists. He does not have to nor needs to discuss His decisions and rulings with anyone. He decides and does it! After all, He created everything by His own good pleasure and will. And when He created, He did not first discuss it with anyone else (except for His Son and the Holy Spirit, who are one with Him).

"Please allow me to use my writer's prerogative and licence to expand with a little more imagery. The book of Hebrews also makes mention of a heavenly country. Thus, it could be that within the heavenly country (or new earth) where the redeemed and saved people of God will live, there would also be a City (New Jerusalem). The city is not the same as the country but fits into the country. A country is not the same as the world or planet but fits into it. So, as we currently have 195 countries in the world that are officially recognized as countries, we might have quite a number of them (each with one or more cities, towns, and communities) in the New Earth where the New Jerusalem is the main capital city where God's throne will be.

Thus, it could easily be that those who, for one or other reason known by God, would live in houses outside of the city, but will be allowed to travel from time to time to visit the city. Consider what Jesus related in Luke 16 when He spoke about the parable of the unjust steward. When an accusation was brought against this steward and he was about to lose his stewardship, he devised a shrewd plan to stay in the game, so to speak. He called all of his master's debtors and gave each of them considerable rebates. Jesus said that the master commended this unjust steward because he dealt shrewdly (some may argue that he dealt wisely; others may say he was cunning). Jesus recommended that the 'sons of light' should learn from this and make friends, through unrighteous mammon, so that they (we) may be received into an everlasting home (see verse 9).

What does this mean in plain English? Jesus told His followers to 'use worldly wealth to gain friends'. In other words, to use their earthly resources to gain friends in order to make a difference in their lives in this world. This parable is certainly not merely for His followers to use their money wisely – that would be too limiting. Every time we give funds to Christian missions around the world, when we feed the hungry and destitute, when we go out of our way to help someone else, it goes a long way in investing in our eternal rest. Sometimes we do not even know the very people that benefit from our benevolence, but what we do touches their lives. God knows it and maybe He will also allow the beneficiaries to see it one day. We cannot gain eternal life by our good works, but good works also count for great rewards nevertheless. Jesus also said that a cup of cold water in His Name will not go unrewarded. For what purpose? So that when life on earth is finished, you will be welcomed into eternal dwellings by your eternal friends. Our 'friends in heaven' could also be those whose lives we have touched on earth in one way or another and would provide places where we could stay from time to time to enjoy eternal joy and companionship.

To further expand on the concepts of eternal cities in the Kingdom of God (New Earth), consider the parable of the minas that Jesus related:

"Then came the first, saying, 'Master, your mina has earned ten minas', and he said to him, 'Well done, good servant; because you were faithful in a very little, have authority over ten cities'. And the second came, saying, 'Master, your mina has earned five minas.' Likewise, he said to him, 'You also be over five cities' (see Luke 19:16-19).

The old argument of whether this should be regarded as figurative or literal comes up again. These cities that Jesus referred to in this parable could well be cities in the literal sense of the word. Scripture on many occasions refers to the new heavens and new earth. Revelation 21 talks about a new earth upon which the New Jerusalem, City of God, will descend from heaven and settle on the new earth. This city will have twelve gates that will never close and will open up into different directions by which the kings of the earth will bring their glory and the honour of the nations into it. These kings will reign over large cities and countries and will be allowed to travel and visit the capital city, New Jerusalem, without any hindrance.

The size of the New Jerusalem will be exceptional and mind-blowing. The city's exact dimensions are measured by an angel and reported to be 12,000 stadia (which, being an ancient Roman or Greek measure of length, measures as one stadium of about 185 meters, originally the length of a stadium). It is the equivalent of 1,400 miles (2,200 kilometres) in length, width, and height (see Revelation 21:17). The angel used a reed as a measurement tool which was according to the measurement of a man (meaning the measurements of humans). This square cube is gigantic, to say the least. It is ten times bigger than France or Germany.

We know through pictures painted for us through the Revelations of John that there will also be rivers, almost similar to those that existed in the Garden of Eden, the first Paradise. The main river (The River of Life) will have trees growing in the middle of its street (or stream), as well as on both sides of this river. The trees will produce twelve different kinds of fruit that will yield their fruit every month. These fruit-producing trees will continually go on to produce fruit on a monthly basis forever and ever.

No one that would be fortunate to be eternal citizens of such a heavenly country will ever be bored. There will be so much to take in and experience that will keep us busy for an eternity. Imagine the different colours, fashions, sounds, countryside, brilliant light, heavenly music and so forth that our current earthly bodies will not be able to absorb or appreciate. It is for these reasons that God will provide us all with special heavenly and celestial bodies – bodies that can travel with the speed of light but would also be able to eat the heavenly fruit. I cannot say whether our new celestial bodies would be wholly dependent on food for its maintenance or not – I do not think so, but we will be able to eat fruit for our enjoyment. God has already orchestrated it. It must still take place at the right time."[66]

In his book *Whatever Happened to the Gospel?*, RT Kendal says: "These things said, we will all learn a lot more about heaven five minutes after we are there than all the preaching, guessing, imagining, writing, and fantasizing might suggest this side of heaven."[6]

Hallmarks of Champions

During a tranquil and peaceful afternoon in our home, whilst my wife and I shared a conversation and enjoyed some drinks and snacks, she noted how happy she was. The discussion and accompanying emotions further developed into somewhat deeper and contemplative expressions of thoughts and insights. I was overcome with emotion and an inner movement that I know was brought about by the inspiration of the Holy Spirit.

It dawned upon me to capture those ideas in written form and prayed that the Holy Spirit lead me further to expand the thoughts for the benefit of others. These inspirational thoughts developed into a theme which would be an encouragement to God's children. We can be compared with champions.

The thoughts expressed hereunder are equally relevant to Christians worldwide of all denominations of the great community of the Christian Church. It should benefit any general Christian believer irrespective of which denomination or congregation they belong to. These thoughts are meant to be an encouragement and support for individual Christians, as well as for The Church of Jesus Christ collectively.

To be a champion means to be a winner, overcomer, soldier, defender, upholder, advocate and victor. The theme is centred in the first five letters of the word champion, namely: CHAMP. This word can be unpacked as follows:
C = Contentment
H = Happiness
A = Appreciation
M = Meekness
P = Peace

CHAMPions: What are the hallmarks of champions? The features described below characterize values and elements that form part of the makeup of champions.

C – Contentment

This element refers to a sense of satisfaction with who we are and what we have. Accepting the state that we are in and dealing with it in the best way we can. Accepting the hand; cards; lot that life has presented us. Resigning to that which God has given us (the good and the bad and the ugly) and counting our blessings day by day.

We must make the most of who we are (our own identity, profile, blond, brunette, blue eyes, brown eyes, African, American, European, Asian, child of God, Christian, Believer, and so on). There is a reason why we were born into a particular body within a particular community and country. With whom we are (parents, children, grandparents, grandchildren, brothers, sisters, husbands, wives, cousins, step-families, friends, and so on).

Where we live (villa, apartment, big house, small house, shack, tent, rentals, ownerships, and so forth). Where we work (own business, public service, private company, unemployed). Where we study. Our own particular health, illness, disability, strength, weakness, gifts, talents, abilities, potential to cope with that which life throws at us now in this given point in time.

We were all given only one natural body – contrary to what some belief systems profess. There are no extra bodies in the closet or wardrobe that we can just take out and put on when the first one is worn out or damaged. We are stuck with what we have. However, we are also very special. There is no one else in this whole world exactly like you – not even if you are one of identical twins.

Only you have your own particular design of fingerprints. No one else of the more than 7 billion people traversing the earth at this specific point in time, or in times past, has them! We must not wish for something or to be somebody else to the extent that it takes our focus away from the current situation, thus making ourselves miserable and depressed.

It does not mean that we should not have dreams and plans, working towards improving our lives. It does mean having faith, hope and inner strength to deal with our own particular mix of situations and conditions. God loves us for who we are – we should also do the same.

We must accept and relish our childhood in God. We must not allow ourselves to be overtaken by doubt or fear about our position, even in the face of much turmoil, uncertainty and change within the church structures. Irrespective of any Christian denomination or group where we find ourselves. The position of the church structure might change owing to adaptation and adjustment to social, political, scientific or technical movements and pressure. As a result of the above changes, strategies, policies, doctrines or other adjustments might likewise also have a bearing on the church structures.

What remains important is that we absorb those changes and make sense of them. However, we remain sure of our own position as children of God. It should only intensify our personal relationship with our God and Redeemer, Jesus Christ. We must draw deeply from our own godly experiences of the past and ensure that Jesus remains the centre of our lives as we proceed into the future. He has chosen us and will not abandon us, even though it may look as if the very ground on which we stand has shifted. Our relationship with God remains intact as we intensify our prayers and strive to experience Him in our everyday lives.

H - Happiness
This feature refers to the sense of joy, gladness, love, lightness, fun, laughter and simplicity that one experiences. This comes and goes at any given point in time, sometimes out of the blue. Often the duration of the experience differs from person to person and the given event or non-event. It means that we are enjoying life, ourselves, relationships, environments, people, animals, flora, rivers, oceans, landscapes and natural creation. Joy and

happiness are the same thing, and we should not play around with semantics.

The operative words are that of enjoyment, passion, enthusiasm or an intensity of pleasure that is sometimes indescribable. It also means that we take pleasure in who we are and things we do that are either free or relatively inexpensive. When you enjoy a drink or good company, really enjoy it. When you drive through the countryside, really enjoy the scenery and vista – take it in with all your senses, see it, touch it, taste it, hear it, smell it. Enjoy the beauty of colours and fashions around us – the flowers, trees, grass…

There is the sense of happiness that we feel in and for ourselves of situations, places and people that touch us. Then there is also the sense of happiness that we experience when we reach out to others less fortunate, who find themselves in one or other need. This service of generosity also extends itself into the afterlife as we pray and intercede for lost souls. The goodness we experience when we are able to help others and give of ourselves in the process also creates a sense of happiness and generosity.

Happiness does not only lie in what we receive, but more importantly in what we give. We do not help others to get any reward, but it nevertheless has its inherent benefits. As long as we are in this earthly vale, the gift of happiness and joy comes and goes – it remains of short duration. Our earthly bodies are not designed to absorb and handle long-lasting spurts and streams of happiness and joy. There are also various levels of joy and pleasure that can still be classified as happiness. There is indescribable joy in the mere fact that we are children of God. *We rejoice that our names are written in heaven[i].*

Happiness is the counterweight of misery, pain, sadness and anxiety which should provide a good balance and diversity in the way we experience life in general. Unfortunately, there is so much pain and misery in the world and very little happiness in relation to it. We know the cause stems out of SIN and its effects. The secret is to create as many small pockets of happiness as we can muster. If we have real contentment, we can find happiness in almost everything we do or experience.

We should have joy and gladness in our human experience, knowing full well we also have it in our godly experience. Let us savour the moment, delve deep within it when we find moments of happiness and endeavour to make it linger on a little longer. Let us practise eternal happiness by cherishing the moments of happiness we are fortunate to have whilst still here on earth.

When we are overcome by joyfulness, let us focus on it as if it is the first and last time that we encounter it.

- Let it not pass us by thoughtlessly.
- Let us breathe life and meaning into it.
- Let us have more fun – there is no law against it.
- Let us smile more.

By smiling, we give our faces something to do. By smiling, we also exude goodness and beauty to people around us, thereby touching them inwardly and sharing some of our blessings of that moment. Smiling often evokes goodness in others who see our smiles and allow them to reciprocate likewise. Smiling warms up often cold and chilly hearts and dispositions. This is a beautiful gift to share that will not impoverish us but juxtapose to the enriching of ourselves and others. Smiling and laughter are the two arms of happiness.

We should also laugh much more. Laugh with abundance. Laugh without restraint. Laugh at life. Laugh at situations, conditions and irony – not at people. Laughter is also good for us, not only mentally, but also physically and spiritually. Happiness is one good fruit of a well-adjusted, balanced and content child of God. I echo what the Apostle Paul said: "Rejoice in the Lord always, I repeat rejoice!".

A - Appreciation

This feature also forms an integral part of being a true champion. When one has a sense of appreciation, one is truly grateful and thankful. One of our church leaders once said: "He who *thinks* thanks". This is in essence what it is all about. We have to think about ourselves, our position in life, our relationships, our possessions, our gifts and talents, and so on.

Appreciation is not the same as contentment. However, it is similar and dissimilar. Appreciation is on a higher level than contentment. Whilst contentment is about an enduring sense of satisfaction and acceptance of ourselves and our situation, appreciation goes deeper. Unfortunately, appreciation is often much more short-lived in duration and focused on a given reason. However, this should not be so. We should also strive to have a lasting sense of appreciation and thankfulness.

The precondition for thankfulness is humility.

It thus follows that pride and arrogance excludes a sense of appreciation. However, humility does not mean allowing oneself to be used as a doormat and being manipulated as if one's opinions or views are irrelevant. On the contrary, being truly humble means to bow to the timely will of God and His Majesty. Understanding His Will and Majesty also prompts and moves one to uphold it and stand up for it – even in the face of controversy, pressure, hostility, rejection and alienation. It takes courage, character and determination to stand up for one's beliefs and convictions. The degree to which we are prepared to stand up for our convictions also alludes to the degree of appreciation and gratitude we express as understanding of the benefits afforded to us by our Benefactor.

We essentially live in a society of 'throw-away' things; instant gratification and ungratefulness. This malaise also pulls through to intangible things such as values, ethics and morality. Having a general sense of appreciation does not come easy to everyone.

It is always a good idea to practise saying 'thank you' for favours, benefits and natural gifts received. We teach this to our children. This should then also be the building blocks to a strong structure and a sense of being thankful and appreciative.

True gratitude and thankfulness come from deep within the heart and soul. Children of God should strive for the feature of appreciation and thankfulness and live a life of gratitude. We do not have enough words of thankfulness for all the natural and spiritual things which we are blessed to have received from God, the true Benefactor and Giver of all good gifts.

Be thankful for everything, small and big, thankful for the breath of life, health and illness, food and drink, children and parents, natural and spiritual gifts, faith and teaching, hope and love for the promise of our eternal inheritance.

As we are appreciative, let us also express this in various ways, such as deep-felt prayer, receiving the Word of God, partaking in the sacrament of Holy Communion. It continues with following, loyalty, fellowship, godly service, dedication, offering and sacrifice. Thankfulness is intertwined with practical measures and is also the key to the heart of the Benefactor. Locked away therein is also the expectation of more to be had from the Benefactor's treasure chest and reserves.

M - Meekness
This element could almost be regarded as an old-fashioned and outmoded word in this modern world wherein we live. What does it mean to be meek? Does meek equate with weak? Certainly not!

Let's start with the Person with whom scripture identifies with the word 'meek'. That is the Person Jesus Christ. One thing is certain – He is certainly not weak! On the contrary, He is absolutely strong and valiant. However, He is also not hard and cold. In fact, He is described as being full of love and mercy. He is soft and compassionate. Thus, there is an inherent dichotomy in the word 'meekness'. It has characteristics of softness, tenderness, gentleness, quietness, obedience, compassion, mercy and love, but also speaks of an inner strength and power.

Meekness also alludes to balance. It certainly does not conjure up images of extremity nor points to either side of the pendulum. It speaks highly of an inner strength and inner control – control of one's emotions, thoughts and actions. It does not mean that one sometimes cannot drift into bouts of despair. Jesus also experienced extreme sadness – so much so that it felt as if the whole world was weighing down on Him.

This happened when He was praying in Gethsemane, moments before His capture, interrogation, trial, false conviction and death sentence. This was indeed also the case spiritually as He felt the full brunt of the world's sin coming upon Him. At another time, He was infuriated when He came into the temple and saw the money-changers and other 'businesses' being conducted. He literally drove them out of the temple saying that His Father's house was a house of prayer and not a den of thieves.

In essence, Jesus was indeed the epitome of meekness and mildness. This inner strength and gift enabled Him to stay true to His commission and purpose on earth. He did not flinch or allow any person or spirit to sway Him towards the left or right. As children of God, we should also possess this spiritual gift of meekness. We should be balanced, tender-hearted and filled with kindness and compassion. However, no one should take us for granted or try to walk over us as if we would not mind. We show the necessary modesty but must stay true to our mission and purpose in life.

When necessary, we must also stand up for what we believe in – our faith and convictions. There is a saying that goes: 'If you do not stand up for something, you will fall for anything!' Our convictions must shine through. We stand up and speak out against those things that threaten our faith and relationship with God. We stand up for godly principles, values and standards – even if it goes against the grain of society and societal norms. We might be blighted, avoided, ostracized or even hated by our contemporaries for that which we believe in. That should not deter us; on the contrary, we are glad that we could suffer for Christ's sake.

Obviously, we are human and also experience the full spectrum of human emotions. We are not spared the trials and tribulations nor the ups and downs of life. We are not shielded in a watertight compartment against the brutality and harshness of life. Life is not (and should not be) a bed of roses. However, we are tested in every circumstance and temptation and, when it happens, we should show what we are made of, what characterizes a true child of God.

This feature of meekness certainly speaks volumes for softness, balance, compassion and inner strength. It places a different spin on the meaning of the word as we encounter it in modern times. There is certainly a place for it and more than just a mere place. It is an essential element of a true champion.

P - Peace
This last feature is certainly not the least. Much has been said and done in the name of peace. However, just like happiness, it is fragile and should be handled with care and consideration. Peace is a desirable condition which promotes stability and growth. It takes place on various levels: personal, inter-personal, in families, groups and communities, countries within its borders, as well as internationally between countries. It goes without saying that it is of utmost importance that personal and inter-personal conditions of peace exist as they form the building blocks of regional and world-wide peace.

The UN (United Nations) adopted Resolution 36/67 to introduce an International Day of Peace which has been observed every year since 21 September 2001. The main purpose is a global day of peace and non-violence. The World Council of Churches (WCC) endorses this resolution and also encourages all church denominations to actively pray for peace on this day and always.

Although Jesus is regarded as the Prince of Peace, He once said that we should keep our own peace and that He will give us His peace – a peace that the world does not know. Peace should be much more than a mere absence of conflict. However, management of conflict certainly helps in creating a more enduring condition of peace. Let's do it one step at a time. Try to find peace within yourself first. It starts with contentment. Accept yourself; accept all that you are – warts and all. Be at peace with yourself. Search and find silence. It is not necessary to try and fill every moment with noise, music, words, people and things.

Next, establish peace within your relationships – peace with your wife, husband, parents, children, siblings, friends and so on. Why is it necessary to fight over seemingly insignificant and small things? The opposite of peace is war – or fighting. People fight for various reasons. Reasons include, but are not limited to rights, perceived injustice, oppression, misunderstanding, greed, avarice, envy and hatred. It is often fuelled by a stubborn selfish stance not to be the least or to give in and capitulate to demands and pressure. Often, we inadvertently hurt the very people whom we (are supposed to) love.

Furthermore, have peace with your church denomination and local congregation. Have peace with the ministers, priests and pastors who serve you even though you might be aware of their faults and mistakes. No one is infallible. Look past them or through them and see our Lord and Saviour serving us. Have peace not only within your local and denominational church, but also with your Christian brethren across the street – meaning those who worship at another church denomination. Do not dislike or hate them – they do not deserve it. They are your brethren as part of the body of Christ. Remember Jesus wants His own to be one in spirit.

We all need the great gathering, fellowship of believers and the collective worshipping of our great God. We need to hear the Word of God; we need to regularly partake of the sacrament of Holy Communion that helps to fashion and cleanse us. Jesus introduced and established the sacrament of Holy Communion and urged His followers to partake of it on a regular basis. He said that if we do not partake of it, we have no part in Him. The Holy Communion also helps us to remember His bitter suffering and death. But, more than that, it helps us to overcome the devil by the Blood of the Lamb and His Word. (see Revelation 12:11).

Find common ground and acknowledge the differences and diversities between us. Everyone cannot be like you (or me), like what you like, value what you value, love what you love and disapprove of what you disapprove of. However, this is where the problem lies. It is not to give an inch, not to give in, not to back down – sometimes even in the face of reason or decency. This smacks of selfishness and arrogance and is quite contrary to true humility and love. This is not the same as standing up for your convictions to advance truths that stand outside yourself, serving to the common good.

- A champion will always strive to search for and find peace.
- A champion will earnestly pray for peace.
- A champion will do his utmost to maintain peace.

At times, it does mean give and take or backing down and retreating at a given point in time in order to advance at a later stage.

When you have peace, you cherish moments of silence and contemplation. In such moments, you listen to your inner thoughts, meditations, and the voice of the Holy Spirit. This is the making of a champion, the making of a wise and great soul and the making and essence of a true child of God. Although the finding and maintaining of worldwide peace may seem ever elusive - within and amongst the champions and children of God, pockets of true peace are certainly attainable. Within this climate of peace, a heavenly atmosphere of stability, strength, warmth and love rules, making room for growth and development.

I hope and pray that you have found some comfort and strength from reading references to thoughts, ideas and insights that contribute to elements of our becoming and being true champions of our God.

I want to hasten by saying that the above is by no means exhaustive or the only thoughts on the subject. This is only what has been revealed to me as I captured it in written form. The general Christian Church is daily bombarded with challenges and threats to its very existence. We should never give up our faith in Jesus and our Heavenly Father. True champions will not give up in their spiritual battles but keep the standard and, with courage, continue the fray. God will take care of us and in due course fulfil the promise of our eternal inheritance.

Further Teachings about The New Jerusalem (by Andrew Maritz)

The triune God can be seen in all that is life. He is Father, Son and Holy Spirit. He is also the Creator, the Divine and Holy One. There are some who ask, "Where is this wonderful God that you are talking about?" but I see Him in everything that man has had no hand in producing. I see Him in everything that holds life.

I see Him in the sun, moon and stars. I see Him in the clouds and the air that I breathe; in the colour of the sky; in the majesty of the oceans and mountains, fascinating living creatures, trees, plants and fruit. I also see God in the amazing makeup of the human body and the human being as a whole.

I see Him in our ability to grasp the abstract; in our ability to love, reason, to communicate with one another, to feel emotion and be fascinated, to imagine and also to dream.

I see our heavenly Father in my brother and sister; in their belief, faith and hope which is real. I see God in the grace and love of Jesus Christ and His teaching. I experience Him in the fellowship of His Holy Spirit. What shall I see in His kingdom?

Christianity is not just a religion or a faith. It is a way of life. My father (natural father), once pointed out that we see the number 'three' appear many times our lives over. He said that human beings are essentially made of three elements which are bone, flesh and blood and then continued to point out that, without eating, drinking and sleeping, the human body would not survive. Some of the threes in Scripture, like Jesus' rising after three days, fascinated me. I then tried to find my own threes and I found that the sun, moon and earth are the clearest terrestrial or heavenly bodies visible to the naked eye. We are always surrounded by air, water and earth (soil) no matter where we are (another three).

The Bible itself shows up many threes (3s) from the Old Testament through to the New Testament. The three men who spoke to Abraham and Sarah on their way to destroy Sodom and Gomorrah. Paul being blinded for three days. Christ vowing to rebuild the temple in three days and resurrecting it after three days. I was thrilled probably more than I should have been when recognising three crosses at the crucifixion of Jesus Christ. There are the sacraments of Holy Baptism, Holy Communion and Holy Sealing, which corresponds to the three in heaven (Father, Son and Holy Spirit). It may appear that fundamentally, life for us earthlings is written in three steps – but we know it is so much more than this. God brings the life, the love, the fascination, imagination and magic to life more than we can see with the human eye. HE WANTS US TO SHARE IN HIS DIVINE LIFE.

"God's actions are aimed at making salvation accessible to mankind. His will to save applies to all people in the past, the present and the future. The history of salvation progresses according to the wise plan of God. The knowledge that God is faithful enables us to confidently wait for the fulfilment of further divine promises (Hebrews 10:23). The doctrine of future things (eschatology) is based on Holy Scripture. Many references to events in the future of salvation history are contained in the gospels and the letters of the apostles. Some key statements are recorded in the Revelations of Jesus Christ, which speak of future things in figurative terms. In this important source of hope for the future, the Lord repeatedly reinforces the promise of His return, reveals the progress of the history of salvation, and thereby grants insights into His future actions." (Catechism NAC, 2012, pg 87-88)

It is no surprise that many parts of the book of Revelation, the final book in Holy Scripture, speaks of the future in figurative terms. We only know what we have seen and experienced on this earth we are living on. The new heaven and earth will also have new things, beings, sights, creations and more than we can imagine now. An indication already to the difference is the promise of a glorified or resurrection body at the rapture when Christ returns (1 Corinthians 15:42-45).

The events and time periods that will follow the return of Christ will ultimately result in the New Jerusalem where true love, peace, joy and righteousness rules for the faithful children of God. Those who continued to believe in Him through life and through the ages and who remained faithful to God will be given this gift of new life. Their faith will become sight - there will be no more need to have faith and no need to hope for a better life. Life will be experienced in its fullness. The earthly Jerusalem was the place where God started His salvation work. The New Jerusalem embodies the completion of this work and eternal life with God, the Father, Son, and Holy Spirit.

Life certainly will be different. The redeemed will be able to see God face to face. They will be able to see His power in action. They will be able to see and grasp the fullness of love, the fullness of His glory and the fullness of life itself. The angel service will be visible. New words will have to be invented to describe the new Jerusalem as words like 'amazing', 'stunning' or 'spectacular' will not suffice as its dynamic will be new, different and out of this world.

The new heaven and new earth described in the book of Revelations is distinctly different from the one we know. There is no sea and sun as well as no night. God Himself illuminates it. The Lamb, Jesus Christ, is its light. In addition to living with their Redeemer and God, the redeemed will also experience life with, in and through God. God the Father, Son, and Holy Spirit will be All in all. With this gift their possibilities will be infinite. Imagine the knowledge that God could share with us. How He creates, designs and shapes things into life. After all, He is the only One who can make something from nothing. Surely, He will satisfy so many questions about the universe and more.

Our joy will be complete. There will be no more sickness, pain, sorrow and suffering to endure. All our hardships and negative experiences will pale into insignificance when we share in His glory. The Holiness of God will rule. The redeemed will live in the truth and the love of God. Life as we now know it will be completely redefined. The age old question to what the meaning of life is will finally, comprehensively and emphatically be answered. An overwhelming thought indeed. How wonderful it will be to hear and see the angelic choir bring praise and honour to God in perfect unison. We can join in. How wonderful it will be to live in perfect unity with our God, our Creator, our Father.

When we will finally understand why He is summed up in only one word – love.

> "And He said to me, it is done!
> I am the Alpha and the Omega, the Beginning and the End. I will give of the fountain of the water of life freely to him who thirsts."[68]

Chapter 12
An inspiring story

On Wednesday, 30 October 2019 while I was driving my car and listening to a Christian radio station broadcast (Radio Tygerberg, channel 104), I was moved by a beautiful story as related by one of the broadcasters.

He related a true story shared with him.

It goes like this:

A father was taken out of this life in 2014 through a tragic car accident. His sudden death left an open wound in the life of his only twenty-year-old daughter. As she struggled to come to terms with his death, she sent him a WhatsApp message on his phone number every day for four years. In her messages, she told him how much she loves and misses him and gave him updates of some events in her life.

Then, four years later, after doing this every day, she received a response from the phone number where she sent all her messages to.

As you can imagine, this really shocked her.

The response message said: 'I am not your father. However, for the past four years, I received your messages and it really kept me going. The same time that you lost your father, I also lost my only daughter through an illness. I could not cope with my loss, but your messages kept me going and sustained me. I did not want to stop you in the past, but now that I feel much better and learned to cope better with my life, I thought I will let you know.

So, the fact that you sent these messages helped us both in dealing with our different losses.

I just want to say that if I was your father, I would be very proud to have you as a daughter. I am sure he loves you where he now finds himself.

If you want to, you can keep on sending me your messages.'

This can only be God!

So, through the perceived tragedies of two people who suffered the loss of loved ones, a beautiful story like this could unfold.

I am also certain that both the departed father, as well as the departed daughter, belonging to two different families, would also rejoice in heaven if they were children of God.

"Greetings and Salutations from Heaven

It was on a cold Sunday, 25 June 1989 directly after divine service that we, as a group of choir members, decided to visit Sister Ewertse, a senior member of our local church in Strandfontein, a suburb of Cape Town, South Africa. She was terminally ill for some time but carried her burden with dignity and patience. Previously, on a few occasions when she was not too weak, another deacon (Cecil Martin) and I would collect her by car. We carried her from her home to the car and from the car into the church. Unfortunately, she did not possess a wheelchair at the time.

On this particular Sunday, as the choir group entered her house, she sat in the lounge to meet us, as it was arranged with her family.

When it was my turn to greet her before we started singing, I was inwardly moved by the Holy Spirit and told her softly that, when she entered the afterlife, to convey my special greetings to our beloved departed friends there. She looked at me seriously but, with a loving and wise demeanour, nodded approvingly by saying, 'Yes, I will certainly do that.'

She passed away the following week.

Life went on and a few years thereafter, in March 1992, we relocated to Vredenburg on the West Coast of the Western Cape, as I secured a lucrative job at a large company.

We lived on the West Coast for about six years after which we moved back to Cape Town.

Many more years went by during which we also immigrated to England and back to Cape Town again.

I almost forgot about my encounter with our dear Sister Ewertse many years before.
Then something amazing happened!

I received heartfelt greetings and salutations from heaven on Friday, 3 June 2016!
But how is this even possible?

The critical, sceptical and human mind will react immediately with dismissals but I am not perturbed. We can only see this with hallowed eyes, pure hearts and faithfulness.

I do not have to convince you of the enormous activity taking place in eternity – all the time, as they do not have to adhere to human inventions of time and space. Time is really relative there. The Apostle Peter reminded us of this:

"But beloved, do not forget this one thing, that with the Lord one day is as a thousand years, and a thousand years as one day."

We believe and know (in our souls) that in the afterlife there is really life and activity, not mere death and inactivity, albeit more in certain quarters and realms than others. We believe this through indications of Holy Scriptures, experiences of faith, the Word of God, and particularly what our Lord and Saviour, Jesus Christ, has taught us.

Likewise, our Christian brethren in heaven also constantly surround us as a cloud of witnesses:

"Therefore, we also, since we are surrounded by so great a cloud of witnesses, let us lay aside every weight, and the sin which so easily ensnares us… looking unto Jesus, the author and finisher of our faith, who for the joy that was set before Him endured the Cross."

They witness our sincerity and faithfulness to God, even (and especially) in the face of controversy, pressures, hardships, struggle…and they also pray for us. They do it constantly (day and night, so to speak, as they have a different conception of time, although they still understand and appreciate our timescales).

So, having said all the above, I now come to the greetings and exaltations that I mentioned earlier.

I received it that morning from the veritable Apostle Paul of all people!

How?
I have a Bible app on my phone whereby I receive daily Bible verses. The verse for that morning reads:

"Salute all the saints in Christ Jesus. *The brethren that are with me* greet you" (Philippians 4:21) [Emphasis added].

This I regarded as a direct and special greeting and salutation from Apostle Paul and our departed redeemed brethren in the heavens to me and also to all my earthly brethren.

They are surrounding us and praying for us. They salute and greet us. This is real Christian love and solidarity in action within the Big Church of Christ encapsulating both the living and the dead (immortal) across different church denominations.

This makes us feel good and strengthened. Both the visible and unseen congregations work from both sides of the River of Life towards the completion of Gods Work!

Even when this greeting came to me in June 2016, I could not connect the dots between that and my previous encounter with Sister Ewertse many years before in 1989, spanning 27 years of earthly time. However, in the light of eternity, it is like a few moments. Only when I started to write the manuscript of this book did it dawn upon me. According to me, sister Ewertse actually did convey my greetings to all my known beloved departed brethren in heaven! This resulted in the Apostle Paul extending their salutations and greetings back to us here on earth.

Amazing isn't it?

I am humbled and thankful for this very personal greeting from heaven and obviously, we want to return the greeting and salutations to them with further support of prayer and intercession.

Greetings my brethren!'[69]

Dream Forecast and Prophesy: 2018

During September 2018 before my wife and I went to Mauritius, I had a vivid dream. I could not understand it fully and could not then make the spiritual connections. However, I did relay it to my wife, Lorraine the next day.

It goes like this:

Both Lorraine and I were walking in Kensington. I remember the area and buildings as I walked it as a child going to school in my growing up years.

I recognized the long road (I think it was Durham road, but not 100% sure). However, in the dream, the road had another name. I looked at the pavement where the names normally appear and it was called "New Road".

So, we continued to walk on this road until it came to 7th Avenue. We then turned down into 7th Avenue until we saw an open field. On the field, we saw some people and a helicopter. We were asked to board the helicopter. It took us to a high mountain and let us out on a level area on the mountain. When we got out, we had to climb up another section to even higher ground to the top.

When we got to the top, we saw a building and when we went in, I noticed a room almost as a classroom where I think we had to write a test. I went through the building to the other side and saw an enchanting forest of beautiful trees. There was also a very large lake with big sized fish that almost jumped out of the water. It looked and felt nice at this place.

We went back through the building and on the other side, we saw many people gathering and just having fellowship. Part of that fellowship involved eating and drinking. I also saw my mother's second eldest sister, 'Tietie Liedeman', who loved me and accepted me almost as her son. She passed away many years before but, here in the dream, she looked happy and serving food at one of the tables.

At one point we were looking down the mountain from the spot where we were and someone said I must go down there on my own, not Lorraine. I said no! I wanted to stay here. But somehow, I could not win the argument.

That is the end of the dream.

I related the dream to Lorraine immediately the next day and we speculated on what it meant.

NOW IN RETROSPECT A YEAR LATER:

I think it means that God had put Lorraine and me on a new path (New Road). This was only a month before we went to Mauritius in October 2018 for a two-week holiday. And one week after we were back from that holiday, Lorraine suffered a severe stroke that left her paralyzed and disabled. She suffered much and experienced much pain. We had her admitted to a number of hospitals and even to a step-down rehabilitation facility. I was unemployed and busy trying to build up a new business, with much turmoil and little success. Six months later, on 14 April 2019, Lorraine died and was promoted and received by God into heaven.

We could not understand why it was in Kensington, but only now did I figure it out. Kensington was the suburb where God had called me many years ago when I was still a teenager, to become a child of His. Also, the new path took us to 7th Avenue. This only has significance to me now. One of our local churches is situated in the vicinity of 7th Avenue.

We had to board on and fly with a pilot in a helicopter – meaning an elevated journey to higher spiritual places.

The high mountain could also mean separation from this world. Still, we had to climb even higher which signifies effort and sacrifice – until we reached the top.

Even on top, we had to write another test in the classroom – for further sanctification and refinement. Also, I saw a beautiful forest with a lake with nice fish that almost jumped from the water. I think it is almost a description of parts of heaven.

What also made it look like heaven were all the people I saw and engaged with, including my favourite aunt, Tietie.

The sad part was that they wanted Lorraine to stay there but said I must go back down the mountain – in other words, that I must leave 'heaven' to go back to earth as my work here is not yet done. I could not argue against it although I tried.

I totally forgot about this dream, which was actually a forecast a year before it happened – really prophetic, as God showed me in this dream what would take place with Lorraine and me in the following twelve months.

I just remembered the dream the evening of Friday, 30 August 2019, whilst preparing to have Lorraine's ashes scattered at her favourite place, overlooking rolling hills towards the sea. Whenever we drove past that particular spot, she always mentioned to me that, if she would pass away before me, that I should scatter her ashes at that place. Just before I fell asleep that evening, the dream came back to me vividly. Amazing!

Thank you, Lord!

Although I am sad that God has called my wife home to heaven, I am very glad and thankful that she has finished her course in the Lord on earth. She was allowed a bed of illness for a short period, but I am convinced that God has extended His grace to her as a final gesture of His love and mercy. God has kept her at my side for thirty-five years. During that time, we raised two sons and taught them the ways of God. Our eldest son is an ordained deacon in our local church and serves the Lord with all his heart. I am sure that our youngest son also strives daily to strengthen his relationship with God. We are very proud of both of them and their families.

CS Lewis, who also lost his wife, had an unusual dream encounter with her. In his book, *A grief observed*, he reflected on that dream the morning after it occurred: "It is often thought that the dead see us. And we assume, whether reasonably or not, that if they see us at all, they see us more clearly than before…"[70]

God also allowed Lorraine and me to travel to many countries and thus have made many friends in those places. Some of them also preceded Lorraine into heaven and now rejoice with her there. Now I also have a very special friend in heaven (with so many others) and, with new vigour, I continue my sojourn on earth, assisting to build the Church of Jesus Christ with the gifts and talents with which He has provided me.

I concur with the wise words of the gifted songwriter, Johan Hermes (1738-1821) in his hymn: "I see in Spirit"

1. I see in spirit, Lord, Your most glorious throne. Could I inherit now this eternal home! Gladly I give You my life completely; in grace, receive me, Lord, into glory!

2. Radiant its beauty for all eternity! That wondrous kingdom mine forever be! Fervent my longing, great is my yearning for that sweet morning of Christ's returning.

3. All thanks I bring You: You blest my eyes to see what joy awaits me where now I long to be. May I be worthy; grant me, Lord, entry into that city to see Your glory![71]

Epilogue

Writing a book like this is not so easy, yet also easy.

What do we mean by this contradiction?

It's not so easy, owing to the fact that we as God's children are expected to be humble and contented in our lives and encounters. After all, the Bible says that God resists the proud, but gives grace unto the humble. And, as humble children of God, we are to take a back seat and be satisfied with our lot. It certainly does not conjure up images of ruling and power.

On the other hand, writing this book also came easily. It is easy and should be understood in the sense that, although we are and should remain humble, we are also called to step forward and take charge of our rightful position in Christ.

Jesus Christ has paid the price.

He came to earth to suffer and give His innocent life as a ransom to buy our freedom from sin and death. Through His victory on the Cross, He paved the way for us as His own to rule with Him.

This ruling or reigning is not only meant to take place one day in the *New Earth* and His eternal kingdom. It starts right now!

We are called to reign with Christ as overcomers with His grace and help. We cannot even dream of any form of reigning in our own strength. We can only do it with and through Jesus. The book of Revelation says:

> "To him who overcomes I will grant to sit with Me on My throne, as I also overcame and sat down with My Father on His throne."[72]

And our rule, as appointed and mandated by God, takes place on different levels. God is and WILL remain the Almighty and ultimate Sovereign Ruler of everything. But He has made us in His image and, through grace and the supreme sacrifice of Jesus, also wants us as His children to reign with Him.

God also equips 'the called' in order for them to rule wisely and with grace. God equips and empowers us as His own with authority over ourselves and our environment. Although God warned Cain, in the beginning, to be careful and not allow sin to rule over him, we all know that Cain ignored this warning. However, we, as His children of the end times, are surely equipped in all areas of our lives. It says in Romans:

> "Therefore, *do not let sin reign* in your mortal body, that you should obey its lusts. And do not present your members as instruments of unrighteousness to sin... For *sin shall not have dominion over you*, for you are not under law but under grace"[73] [Emphasis added].

Further, we as God's children are wise if we at all times heed the wisdom expressed in Revelation 12:11, how to overcome the accuser: "And they overcame him by the blood of the Lamb and by the word of their testimony."

As alluded to in this book, we should first of all rule over ourselves. This is difficult but possible. We should rule over our thoughts, emotions, behaviour, within our marriages and families, within the community and environment, within our finances, businesses and investments, and over demons, forces and circumstances. We are born of royal blood. That is, the Blood of Jesus!

> "Behold, I give you the authority to trample on the serpents and scorpions, *and over all the power of the enemy*, and nothing shall by any means hurt you"[74] [Emphasis added].

Let's lift ourselves up with a new perspective and vision.

Let's walk tall and look everyone straight in the eye – we have nothing to be ashamed of.

Let's impact this current world with the gifts, talents, capabilities, faith and love that God has blessed us with.

Let's trust God to guide us further as His representatives on earth to reveal His will and plan for our fellow man.

Let's remember that God has (already) blessed us and will continue to bless us in future:

> "Blessed be the God and Father of our Lord Jesus Christ, *who has blessed us* with every spiritual blessing in the heavenly places in Christ"[75] [Emphasis added].

So, we are blessed to rule now in this world, and we will also (continue) to rule in God's eternal kingdom in positions and roles that He will assign to us eternally.

Don't shrink and crumble into a miserable lump at small corners. We are not to shrink back into perdition! He that is within us is greater than he who is in the world. We have all the resources of heaven at our disposal if we can just see this and believe it with all our hearts.

We must take charge with faith and grace. This is a great responsibility.

We are also expected to respect the rules and ordinances that God has given us. This is where true obedience stems from. This book is also about the different rules that God has provided to help us navigate our way through life and faith. Rules provide order and security to all who keep to them. The most profound rules or commandments God has given His own through Jesus Christ is to love God above everything, and our neighbour as ourselves.

Part of the rules Jesus wants His own to follow is to exercise true love and unity within the Church of Jesus Christ. He is, after all, the Head of His Church. We are all members of the same Church and Body of Christ. Let us harness this unity and love and not bring about separation and division. Let us strive to rise above denominational boundaries. Let us not vie amongst one another to overshadow our fellow churches in pettiness and doctrinal superiority.

Let's absorb into our souls and spirits what Apostle Peter said about us:

> "But you are a chosen generation, a royal priesthood, a holy nation, His own special people, that you may proclaim

the praises of Him who called you out of darkness into His marvellous light; who once were not a people but are now the people of God, who had not obtained mercy but now have obtained mercy."[76]

It gives the Triune God immense joy and satisfaction when Father, Son and Holy Spirit see how we, as God's own, rise up and rule with grace and truth (and with full authority) in the different positions we are currently occupying on earth. This is a prelude for what is to come.

We are to walk with love and joy.

We are to praise and thank God continuously.

We, who are loving the Lord, are called to the following, according to this hymn, as expressed by the songwriter, Isaac Watts (1674-1748):

Chorus:
We're marching to Zion
Beautiful beautiful Zion!
We're marching upward to Zion
The beautiful city of God!

Verses:
Come ye that love the Lord
And let your joys be known
Join in a song with sweet accord
And thus surround the throne

The God that rules on high
That all the earth surveys
That rides upon the stormy sky
And calms the roaring seas

The hill of Zion *yields*
A thousand sacred sweets
<u>*Before*</u> *we reach the heavenly fields*
Or walk the golden streets

There we shall see His face
And never, never sin
There from the rivers of His grace
Drink endless pleasures in[77]
[Emphasis added]

Notes

Prologue
1. Revelation 3:21
2. James 1:12
3. Luke 19:17
4. Genesis 1:28
5. Genesis 4:7
6. Psalms 145:13
7. Matthew 22:37-40

Chapter 1
8. Galatians 5:22-23 KJV
9. Proverbs 23:7
10. Philippians 4:8
11. NAC Hymnal, Uberlandstrasse 243, Zurich, 2008, Hymn 300, *Softly and tenderly*)

Chapter 2
12. https://www.collinsdictionary.com/dictionary/english/emotion
13. John 2:15
14. Matthew 9:36
15. Matthew 26:37,38
16. Jeremiah 17:9-10
17. Matthew 15:19-20
18. Ephesians 4:26
19. Proverbs 4:23
20. Philippians 4:7
21. Genesis 4:6
22. Colossians 3:15

Chapter 3
23. Colossians 4:6
24. James 3:3-5
25. Ephesians 4:29-32
26. 1 Timothy 3:2-7
27. Romans 12:1-2
28. 2 Corinthians 7:1

Chapter 4
29. https://www.guinessworldrecords.com/world-records/highest-divorce-rate
30. www.statssa.gov.za/?p=11192June4,2018

31. Ephesians 5:31,33
32. Hebrews 13:4
33. Daniel 7:23-27
34. RE Haridien, *The Mystery of 1*, (Durban, South Africa: We publish 4U, Pinetown Printers, 2018), 69-74

Chapter 5

35. https://family.lovetoknow.com/about-family-values/types-family-structures
36. Colossians 3:18-21

Chapter 6

37. Luke 12:32 KJV
38. Genesis 1:31 KJV
39. James 3:16 KJV
40. Proverbs 28:22
41. Matthew 5:5

Chapter 7

42. Revelation 20:6
43. http://en.wikipedia.org/wiki/Community
44. Ephesians 6:12
45. Romans 12:2

Chapter 8

46. Psalm 8:5
47. John 14:6
48. John 14:16-17

Chapter 9

49. Genesis 1:28-31
50. Genesis 3:17-19
51. https://en.wikipedia.org/wiki/Industrial_Revolution

Chapter 10

52. https://showme.co.za/pretoria/business/9-steps-to-starting-your-own-business/
53. Genesis 14:23
54. Genesis 30:27
55. Genesis 30:31-32
56. Genesis 30:43
57. RE Haridien, *The Mystery of 1*, (Durban, South Africa: We publish 4U, Pinetown Printers, 2018), 64

Chapter 11

58. Psalms 103:19-22
59. Psalms 145:13
60. Ephesians 1:3-6
61. *The Genius of Albert Einstein: His Life, Theories and Impact on Science* by Elizabeth Howell August 15, 2019, Science & Astronomy

62. 2 Peter 3:8
63. *No time*, Poem by Helen Steiner Rice, 1984
64. Revelation 21:9-10
65. https://www.christianity.com/theology/what-does-the-phrase-god-is-sovereign-really-mean-11555729.html
66. RE Haridien, *The Mystery of 1*, (Durban, South Africa: We publish 4U, Pinetown Printers, 2018), 123-127
67. RT Kendall, *Whatever happened to the Gospel?* (Lake Mary, Florida: Charisma House, 2018), 159
68. Revelation 21:6

Chapter 12
69. RE Haridien, *The Mystery of 1*, (Durban, South Africa: We publish 4U, Pinetown Printers, 2018), 97-101
70. CS Lewis, *A Grief Observed,* (New York: HarperOne, 2015), 70
71. *I see in spirit*, NAC Hymnal Uberlandstrasse 243, CH – 8051 Zurich, Switzerland, 2008, Hymn 413
Epilogue
72. Revelation 3:21
73. Romans 6:12-14
74. Luke 10:19
75. Ephesians 1:3
76. 1 Peter 1:9-10
77. *Come ye that love the Lord*, NAC Hymnal, Uberlandstrasse 243, Zurich, Switzerland, 2008, Hymn 406

Another book written by Richard Haridien is listed below:

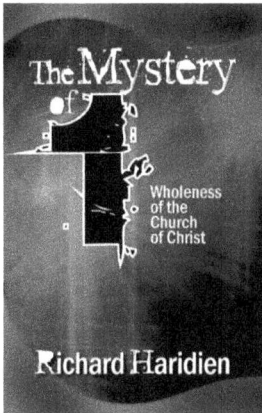

The main purpose of this book is a clarion call to the Global Church to foster unity and love among each other that should be hallmarks of true children of God.

Even as we speak our brethren are persecuted in certain parts of the world. The Church of Christ is called to support and pray for them. We should feel with them as we are also indirectly affected. We should further stand in solidarity and transcend denominational boundaries instead of being divisive by trying to prove our rightness or doctrinal superiority over each other. This is the time for true unity and love!

_____